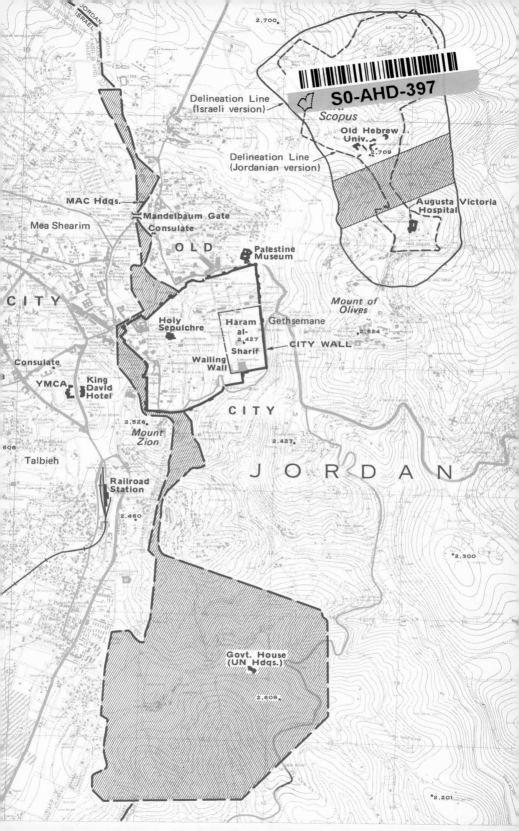

S0-AHD-397

2.700

Delineation Line
(Israeli version)

Scopus

Old Hebrew
Univ.
2.709

Delineation Line
(Jordanian version)

Augusta Victoria
Hospital

MAC Hdqs.

Mea Shearim

Mandelbaum Gate
Consulate

O L D

Palestine
Museum

C I T Y

Holy
Sepulchre

Haram
al- 2.427
Sharif

Gethsemane

*Mount of
Olives*

2.624

CITY WALL

Wailing
Wall

CITY WALL

Consulate

YMCA

King
David
Hotel

C I T Y

2.526

*Mount
Zion*

2.427

Talbieh

Railroad
Station

J O R D A N

2.460

2.300

Govt. House
(UN Hdqs.)

2.608

608

2.300

2.201

DISCARDED

JERUSALEM, KEY TO PEACE

This volume is the second
of a series published by
The Middle East Institute

in honor of the late

JAMES TERRY DUCE

from the proceeds of

THE JAMES TERRY DUCE MEMORIAL FUND

established in honor
of the Institute's President
1961-1963

▼

The Members of the Board of Governors of
The Middle East Institute
are the Trustees of the Fund

Jerusalem, Key to Peace

by

Evan M. Wilson

THE JAMES TERRY DUCE MEMORIAL SERIES

VOLUME II

THE MIDDLE EAST INSTITUTE

Washington, D. C.

1970

Upsala College
Library
East Orange, N. J.

915.694

W747j

123103

Copyright @ 1970 by The Middle East Institute
Library of Congress Catalogue Card Number 70-119026

Printed in the United States of America
by French-Bray Printing Company, Baltimore, Md.

iv

FOR LEILA

Table of Contents

List of Maps

List of Illustrations

List of Appendices

Foreword

The writing of this book has been urged on me by a number of people, in and out of the United States government, who are familiar with my particular background on the Arab-Israel problem. This experience goes back more than twenty-five years and culminates in a three-year tour as US Minister and Consul General at Jerusalem, before, during, and after the June 1967 war. It was suggested to me that my observations while at Jerusalem, our only Foreign Service post having contacts on both the Arab and the Israeli side, were unique. Taken with my earlier background, these experiences would be worth recounting as a basis for advancing some thoughts on the present and future handling of the problem of Jerusalem proper, as well as the wider issues still in dispute.

My suggestions for the future are made in the hope of contributing to a solution of this critical and baffling problem. My aim has been to be completely objective, in so far as this is humanly possible. Therefore I fully realize that my conclusions will be pleasing to neither the Arabs nor the Israelis. The views set forth are wholly my own and I take full responsibility for them.

This work is not intended to be another diplomatic memoir or another account of the June War. Nor is it a scholarly history of the Palestine problem, although considerable attention is devoted to the background, so essential for an understanding of the current impasse. The student of the Middle Eastern scene will find the bibliography, appendices, maps and notes to be of use in pointing to directions in which further studies can be pursued.

In preparing a work of this nature it is virtually impossible to record my thanks to all those who have given me help and inspiration. I would like, however, to express my appreciation to several colleagues in the Department of State and the Middle East Institute who read the manuscript at various stages and made helpful suggestions. Mention of the Institute prompts me to submit that it is fitting to have this book as the second publication in the Middle East Institute's James Terry Duce Memorial series. This is particularly true in view of Mr. Duce's lifelong devotion to the cause of peace in, and understanding of, the Middle East.

Finally, I would like to thank Mrs. Alice VanEss Brewer for her assistance in preparing the manuscript and Mr. R. David Wert for designing and preparing the maps.

Evan M. Wilson

Washington, D. C.
October, 1969

I

Introduction: Life In Divided Jerusalem

A Dome, a Tomb and a Wall; a Crescent, a Cross and a Star; three faiths, three worlds, three ways of life: such was the setting for our life in the Holy City.

Two homes, two offices, two sets of friends; two cultures, two nations at war: such was the pattern of our daily life in Jerusalem.

While the life we led brought us many problems, it gave us an unparalleled opportunity to follow developments on both sides of the Armistice line between Israel and the Arabs (see map 1). Ours was the only Foreign Service post that was in contact with both Arabs and Israelis. As Consul General in Jerusalem it was my responsibility to report on the situation throughout my consular district, which comprised the entire city of Jerusalem and the West Bank of the Jordan, and to maintain close contact with United Nations Headquarters in Jerusalem. Because of the city's importance as an ecclesiastical center I was also expected to keep in touch with its many religious leaders. I was independent of the Ambassadors at both Tel Aviv and Amman and reported direct to the Secretary of State.

To this assignment I brought a background of some twenty-five years' familiarity with Jerusalem and the Palestine question. During my four years on the State Department's Palestine desk, following a tour of duty in Cairo, I had spent some time in the area in 1946 while serving as secretary to the Anglo-American Committee of Inquiry. I had gained further experience of the whole complex of Arab-Israel issues during subsequent assignments to London, to the Department of State's Policy Planning Staff, and to Beirut, before coming back to Jerusalem in 1964.

From the time my wife, Leila, and I arrived in Jerusalem until the outbreak of the war in June 1967, we led an extraordinary and complicated life. The city, like Berlin, was divided, but the difference was that the United States had diplomatic relations with the governments on both sides of the Jordan-Israel Armistice line, which divided the city (see end papers). I had to maintain two offices, one in the Israeli and one in the Jordanian sector, although I was Consul General for all of Jerusalem and the two offices were theoretically integral parts of a single establishment.

The reason for this was that officially Jerusalem was regarded by the United States, by most of our Western allies, and by many resolutions of the United Nations, as a single, undivided and international city, even though this status has never come into actual being.

The upshot was that we consular officers in Jerusalem had to operate on both a *de jure* and a *de facto* basis. *De jure*, we were accredited, if that term may be used for so loose an arrangement, to an entity (the *corpus separatum* as it was termed in the basic resolution of the UN General Assembly—see map 2) which did not exist. *De facto*, we had to recognize the occupation of the two halves of the city by the Israelis and Jordanians, respectively, in order to be able to function at all. It could be said that whenever we passed through the checkpoints at Mandelbaum Gate, as we did several times a day, and waved at the Israeli and Jordanian border policemen, we were according them *de facto* recognition. In all our official acts, however, we were under instructions scrupulously to avoid doing anything that would imply a recognition of the sovereignty in the city of the two countries involved. Thus we always used "Jerusalem" as our official address, not "Jerusalem, Israel" or "Jerusalem, Jordan." The maintenance of this posture naturally required considerable mental agility, not to say hair splitting, on the part of the Consular Corps—especially in connection with the Israelis, who regarded their part of Jerusalem as their capital.

This, however, was only one of the aspects of our daily existence that partook of an Alice in Wonderland quality. We had two local staffs who never met, two separate wage scales, two currencies, and two standards of living. My wife and I even had to maintain two residences, two sets of friends, and two sets of social engagements. Our life was truly a tale of two cities. Of the members of our staff, only the American commissioned officers could cross freely back and forth between the two halves of the city. To maintain contact between our two offices (only five or six minutes apart) we carried written messages from one side to the other—this was the only way our Israeli and Jordanian employees could communicate at the time I arrived. Later we installed a most useful two-way radio, which was also to prove invaluable during the June War.

Whenever we went from one sector to the other, we passed from one to the other of two hostile jurisdictions, which were officially at war with one another, since only an armistice, not a peace treaty was in effect. The iron curtain separating the two sectors was complete: there was no telephone, no mail service, no commercial traffic of any kind. Each sector had its own water supply and its own power: the Jordanians had had to install these after the 1948 Palestine war, since both water and electricity had previously been furnished from what became the Israeli side.

The symbol of the divided life we led was the Mandelbaum Gate, which played so prominent a rôle in our daily lives and which was the only official crossing point between the two sectors. Strictly speaking, it was not a gate at all, but a crossroads in the middle of no-man's land, adjoining the house, in ruins since 1948, of a merchant named Mandelbaum. The Israeli and Jordanian checkpoints were about two hundred yards apart and we would often see crowds of tourists assembling or changing cars or buses in the no-man's land, or walking from one checkpoint to the other (vehicles from one sector were not permitted to enter the other).

The Jordanian and Israeli checkpoints were maintained by border police who were uniformly courteous and helpful to us. They always waved us on through and never asked for the variety of passes and permits that we had to carry. Interestingly enough, the two detachments wore the same uniform, a carryover from the days of the British Palestine Police. Another hold-over was the use of horses by the Israeli, but curiously enough not the Jordanian, police—one would have expected it to be the other way round. At 8:00 p.m. the army took over and all traffic stopped.

At intervals of perhaps a month two officials from either side who dealt with matters affecting Mandelbaum Gate crossings would meet in the middle of the Mandelbaum Square to iron out some technical point (they talked in Arabic). There was no other contact between the two sides, except each morning when a Jordanian and an Israeli policeman would meet in the Square and exchange bundles of newspapers for the use of their respective governments.

The unlimited crossing privilege was enjoyed by career consular officers, by members of the United Nations Truce Supervision Organization (UNTSO), and by the heads of ecclesiastical establishments. The crossing privilege was extended to our families. Tourists and other private citizens of foreign countries were allowed to cross in one direction only, although we could arrange round-trip crossings for official travellers, including Senators and Congressmen. Neither Jordanians nor Israelis were permitted to cross, with the exception of limited numbers of Christians from Israel who were permitted to go over to the Jordanian side to worship at Christmas and Easter. About 60,000 tourists and other private individuals made the one-way crossing each year, mainly from the Jordanian to the Israeli side as this made for fewer visa problems—persons with Israeli notations of any kind in their passports were not admitted to certain Arab countries. For this reason, incidentally, we consuls carried two passports: one for Israel and one for the Arab states.

The members of the Consular Corps were allowed to drive their cars between the two sectors, using special license plates. This was a great convenience, although I had to keep two drivers, one on each side, and drive the car through the Gate myself. Our special plates were theoretically to be used only in the area of the proposed international city of Jerusalem, so we also had both Jordanian and Israeli plates, which in actual practice were seldom used.

In describing the two sectors we habitually used the expression "New City" for the Israeli sector and "Old City" for the Jordanian sector. This caused some confusion as the term "Old City" is also used at times to mean the Walled City of Jerusalem, which was wholly within the Arab or Jordanian sector. As our principal building, a superb old Arab house containing both the office and residence which had been occupied by my predecessors for the past fifty years, had fallen to the Israeli sector when the demarcation line was drawn after 1948, our government had leased a building in the Old City right by Mandelbaum Gate which was likewise both an office and a residence. It was customary, since the Consul General had his principal place of residence in the Israeli sector, for the next ranking officer to live in the Jordanian sector. Our other Americans were divided more or less evenly between the two parts of the city and naturally enough tended to have their main contacts with the residents of their home sector. It was only the Consul General and his wife who were called on to maintain extensive contacts in both sectors. In view of the fact that the gate was closed between 8:00 p.m. and 8:00 a.m. every day, we had to spend the night in the Old City whenever we had an evening engagement there. For this purpose we used a small one-room apartment with kitchenette and bath on the ground floor of our Old City building. It was here and in the adjoining patio and garden, usable about six months of the year, that we did our entertaining of Old City friends.

Living this kind of life gave rise to a number of problems in the logistical field, especially with regard to entertaining. As our home base was in the Israeli sector, whenever we were going to entertain in the Jordanian sector we had to prepare the meal, transport it and the linen and silver to the Old City, hire someone to serve, and bring back the leftovers. This cumbersome procedure placed a considerable burden on the lady of the house, who on these occasions would make a number of trips back and forth between our two buildings—an operation that was time-consuming and sometimes frustrating as there was almost always something that had been forgotten.

It can readily be imagined that with a set-up so unusual and so complicated as this, there should be considerable confusion and uncertainty on the part of our many visitors and correspondents as to the actual status on the ground.

In one instance a Very Important Person wrote that he was coming to the Old City and staying at the Inter-Continental Hotel, then moving the next day to a hospice on the Mount of Olives. Since the Inter-Continental itself is on the Mount of Olives, this puzzled us until the gentleman arrived and explained that what he had in mind was the Mount of the Beatitudes (in northern Israel, above the Sea of Galilee) where there happens to be a hospice used by travellers. Lesser confusions, as to the location of this or that particular Holy Place, or its significance, were almost daily occurrences. We often wondered just what impression our visitors got of Jerusalem as they were whisked from one shrine to another to the accompaniment of an endless but not always very comprehensible stream of patter from their guides. One time, Leila recalls, she was taking a Senator around the Church of the Holy Sepulchre, and after she had explained that this was the site of the Crucifixion and Resurrection, he asked in a puzzled way: "Just what was it you said happened here?"

One of my favorite stories is about the lady with the harp. A well-known professional harpist from the United States wrote me at our Consulate in the Old City, saying that she planned to give a recital in the Old City, cross into the New City and give another recital there. She wanted to know if we could help with the problem of transporting her harp through the Mandelbaum Gate. After checking with the authorities on both sides, I replied that unfortunately this would not be possible. There were no facilities for making shipments through the Gate and, in any event, the authorities declined to make an exception in her case. Shortly thereafter, I received a letter at my other office in the New City from the same lady, saying she had had a most unhelpful letter from a Mr. Wilson, the Consul on the Arab side, and asking if I could help her with him!

It was inevitable that our local contacts on either side of the line, being unable to follow us across to the other side, should tend to be suspicious of what we did as soon as we got through the Mandelbaum Gate. That we should be regarded as suspect by each side and that our Israeli friends should consider us pro-Arab and our Arab friends consider us pro-Israeli, was understandable. It might even be said that this helped contribute to the attitude of impartiality that was called for by United States policy, and that we tried so hard to maintain. The result, however, was to make our position a highly unenviable one.

To a considerable extent the same attitude toward us was reflected by our own Embassy staffs in Tel Aviv and Amman. It was natural for the members of each Embassy to see things as their host country did and to regard us, because we were in daily contact with the people on the other side of the fence, as tainted. Since neither Israel nor Jordan accepted the international status of Jerusalem, members of the two Embassies had to tread warily to avoid offending the susceptibilities of their hosts on the one hand, or, on the other, contravening the formal US government position that Jerusalem was an international city. Years before, a careful set of procedures had been worked out to govern the relations between the three offices and to prescribe who should call on whom locally and the like. Fortunately the two Ambassadors in question were personal friends as well as Foreign Service colleagues of long standing and this helped keep things on an even keel, although problems did arise from time to time.

The fact that the Israelis had declared Jerusalem to be their capital and had moved nearly all of their government departments there meant that our Ambassador and his staff had to travel about an hour and a half from Tel Aviv to see officials who were only around the corner from the Consulate General but who did not recognize us officially because we personified the concept of an international Jerusalem. It also meant that when important visitors from Washington, such as an Assistant Secretary of State or a Senator, came to Jerusalem to call on high-ranking Israeli officials, they were not brought into contact with us, nor were we included in any entertaining for them. These visitors to Israel thus were not given any opportunity to be briefed by the only Foreign Service post having contacts with both parties to the dispute.

There were, of course, certain local Israeli officials with whom the Consular Corps was in contact. But it was awkward to be cold-shouldered by the Israeli government and disappointing, to an officer like myself with friends in the Israeli government service, to be deprived of all official contact with them.

Many of our VIPs were going through the Mandelbaum Gate, and all arrangements for this were in our hands, since members of the two Embassies could not cross to the other side without applying for special permission which was only granted at infrequent intervals. We also provided assistance to those of our visitors who were interested in sightseeing in the Old City, where most of the historic shrines are located, and in shopping for rosaries, crowns of thorns, bottles of Jordan river water, and similar souvenirs. Occasionally I would give a briefing to these visitors to the Old City but these opportunities were comparatively rare.

Jerusalem was an excellent base for trips into the countryside and we travelled extensively on both sides, not just for recreation but to get acquainted with the two very different cultures represented by Israel and the Arab world. In Jordan, we often went down to the Jordan valley, to explore the East Ghor Canal, the Mukhaybah dam site, and the refugee camps. The East Ghor Canal, built in the lower Jordan valley for the purpose of bringing sweet water to the region, was an essential for the agriculture of the valley because of the highly saline nature of the Jordan river in its lower reaches. The Mukhaybah dam was intended to serve the same purpose by increasing the flow of water into the canal from the Yarmuk, which forms the border between Syria and Jordan and is the principal tributary of the Jordan. These water projects of the Jordanian government figured prominently in our American aid program and represented a very considerable tech-nological achievement—now a casualty of the war and the postwar fighting in the valley.

One of the most beautiful views in all Jordan is at Umm Qays, high on the hills above the Sea of Galilee and the reputed place where the Gadarene swine rushed into the sea. In Roman times it was the site of a great university city and there are the remains of no less than three Roman theaters still to be seen. From there we could look across at the Israeli border settlements and follow the course of the Israeli canal (known as the National Water Carrier), which takes water from the lake down to the coastal plain. We could also see the conspicuous "saline effluent" canal which takes salt water from certain springs in the lake and conveys it into the Jordan river at the point where it enters Jordanian territory, rendering the river unusable for irrigation at certain seasons.

Once one's imagination has been captivated by the desert, its exploration is irresistible. We frequently took trips there, going camping with Arab friends at Azraq, east of Amman, to explore the eighth century desert castles of the Umayyad Caliphs, and visiting the Crusader castle at Kerak, a magnificent site towering over the Dead Sea, four thousand feet below, with stupendous views.

We also travelled all over Israel, getting the feel of the vibrant life of the country and also seeing its historical treasures. We climbed the rock of Masada, recently excavated by Israeli archaeologists and the scene of historic Jewish resistance against the Romans. In the summers we often swam at the beaches on the Mediterranean coast although it was always refreshing to get back to the cooler altitude of Jerusalem (some 2,500 feet). We swam most often at Ashqelon, home town of Delilah, where the proprietor of the Dagon Hotel, Mr. Dorot, regaled us with fascinating tales about the early days of the Jewish settlers in Palestine and gave us many insights into contemporary Israeli society.

A favorite haunt was Tiberias, a beautiful lake with its Biblical associations and a scene of rest and quiet, even if the Syrian military positions seen directly across the lake were a constant reminder of the grim realities of the present. From Tiberias we visited Galilee and the upper Jordan valley. We drove along the border of Lebanon, which we had previously known from the other side, and visited Acre of the Crusaders. In the Negev, in the arid south, we saw Avdat and Shivta, two outstanding archaeological sites, thriving at such different periods as 6,000 years ago, 2,000 years ago and the fourth century A. D.

On both sides we went looking in early spring for the wild flowers that made the countryside so lovely, and we pursued our search for the Byzantine mosaics which abound in the whole area and which were one of the most precious legacies of the past in both Israel and Jordan.

My wife was constantly involved with our other consular wives in activities designed to get them to know more about the two civiliza-tions in which we moved. Making it a point to alternate between Israeli and Jordanian interests, they visited and worked with welfare and cultural organizations, called on artists in their studios, and examined the fabulous manuscripts and other art objects belonging to religious centers or private collectors. Leila's most rewarding activity lay in teaching classes in art appreciation in girls' schools on both sides. Sometimes she went to the school and sometimes the girls came to one or the other of our two homes for relaxed conversation over our collection of art books.

One of the less pleasant aspects of life in Jerusalem was that the Holy City seemed to attract crackpots of all kinds. In over thirty years' experience in the Foreign Service I had never had a post where there were so many mental cases. Our officers became accustomed to being called up in the middle of the night by someone who had a plan for preserving the peace of the world and wanted it brought to the President's attention at once. One problem peculiar to our local situation was that many of these people seemed obsessed with the idea of getting across the Armistice line. On three different occasions we had to deal with an American resident of the Israeli sector with a history of mental illness who managed to get through the no-man's land, with its barbed wire and mines—an extremely dangerous thing to do—only to be picked up each time by Jordanian patrols, jailed for a few days, and released to us through the Mixed Armistice Commission.

A basic feature of our life in Jerusalem that we came to accept was that our position there was essentially a very tenuous one, since either of the two local governments could at any time withhold permission for the consuls to cross at Mandelbaum Gate and thus prevent us from operating our offices as single units. Indeed, the whole background against which we lived was one of instability: tension along the Armistice lines, occasional shooting incidents, sabotage raids, reprisals, sometimes actual warfare, with intervals of relative quiet. In late 1966 and early 1967 these tensions increased markedly until finally war came again.

All in all, the most difficult feature of Jerusalem for us was the schizophrenic aspect of the life we led. We went back and forth daily, sometimes several times a day, between two different worlds—and to do this, and maintain the impartiality that was expected of us by our government (though not by either party to the dispute) required the ability to shift mental gears rapidly. Frequently, depending on the vagaries of our schedule, we would find ourselves first with one group, Arab or Jewish as the case might be, and then within a very few minutes, with the other—with people who had never met the first ones, or at least not for nineteen years, and who knew practically nothing about them.

The June War of course drastically altered the pattern of our daily living. It had a traumatic effect on us, for we had the unusual experience of seeing one-half of our friends occupied militarily by the armed forces of the other half. Our unique situation did, however, make it

possible for us to be of service in the period immediately following
hostilities, since we had contacts on both sides of the line.

A final commentary on our life in Jerusalem is that in spite of all
the difficulties and frustrations we experienced, the Holy City had the
capacity to fascinate and to charm more than any other place we have
known. We have been under its spell ever since we first saw it in 1939,
and we always will be. "If I forget Thee, O Jerusalem, let my right
hand forget her cunning." It was perhaps because we loved the city
and all of its people so much that the events of the war had such a
traumatic effect on us.

II

The Setting

It is said the medieval pilgrims would fall on their knees and rend their garments in an excess of spiritual ecstasy when they first caught sight of Jerusalem from one of the surrounding hilltops after their arduous climb from the ancient Mediterranean ports of Jaffa or Acre. Such indeed is the spectacular location of the Holy City on the crest of a ridge along the skyline that even today the most prosaic visitor must pause and gaze in wonder. From whatever direction the city is approached, one must go up to it. The hills rise and fall away in every direction; in the words of the Psalmist, they "stand about Jerusalem: even so standeth the Lord round about his people, from this time forth for evermore."

The city that has gripped the imagination of men for so many centuries is the Walled City of Jerusalem as it still exists today, surrounded by more modern quarters. The city walls, winding along the ridges and across the ravines, the honeycombed houses, the ancient stone buildings, are like the hills themselves, pale in color, almost white in the glare of noontime, but yellow, gold, pink, even purple as the sun's rays shift and evening comes. The clear mountain air and the reflected glow from the endless desert to the east combine with sun and sand and stone to create an indescribable luminosity over the whole landscape. The Western eye, accustomed to the greens, blues and browns of more fertile and more forested lands, is immediately struck by this strangely arresting light and by the paleness of the color. The effect has been remarkably caught by the nineteenth century British artist David Roberts, whose aquatints of the city and its surroundings are prized by all who have lived there. It was Roberts' contemporary, the pre-Raphaelite painter Thomas Seddon, who, writing from Jerusalem in midsummer, described it thus:

> At present, the color varies singularly. Whenever the light shines directly on them, the hills look white, with lines of yellow running over them from the dry parched herbage; but when the sun is low, so that the sides of the rocky ledges are in shadow, the hill is of a glorious purple, mixed with the

11

golden and brown tints of the herbage. The white rock is also very susceptible of color, from the rays of the morning or evening sun, and the little earth that is visible being reddish. The Mount of Olives every evening is of a wonderfully beautiful, rather red purple. (Page 158, "Places" in the series People, Places and Things. London: Grosvenor Press, 1954).

Against the rocky background of the land the spring flowers brought out by the winter rains in wild and brilliant profusion are a sight never to be forgotten. White or pink cyclamen seem to sprout from every crevice. Scarlet anemones are followed by tulips and poppies and ranunculus, providing a sharp accent to the scene, in contrast to the countless varieties of hard-to-see, enchanting little orchids. Later come the black iris, the brilliant blue lupin on the higher slopes. As summer approaches, acres of golden daisies and thick growths of tiny phlox give added color to whole hillsides, before all is burned off by the intense heat, unbroken by rain day after day from May to November. No wonder Disraeli, in Tancred, called Jerusalem in summer "a city of stone in a land of iron with a sky of brass."

I speak of summer heat and winter rain (there is rarely snow), but I recall that the tenth century Muslim writer Muqaddasi likened the climate to that of Paradise—neither too hot nor too cold. With this I would agree. The days are hot, it is true, for some six months and extremely dry, but at 5:30 in the afternoon, almost as though a bell had rung, a breeze comes up. Indeed it is so cool after sunset that we could seldom sit in our garden in the evenings.

While the setting of the Holy City is thus one of great beauty, it is not this alone that has made Jerusalem one of the great cities of the world. There is another aspect to its peculiar quality that led the mapmakers of the Middle Ages to place the city at the center of the universe and that has made Jerusalem the goal of travellers and pilgrims for centuries. I refer, of course, to its associations, religious and historical.

Jerusalem is unique for the reason that the three great monotheistic religions of the world—Judaism, Christianity and Islam—all look to it as their Holy City. Their interests are focussed on one particular site, which happens to be, tradition tells us, where Abraham prepared to sacrifice Isaac, Solomon built his Temple, Our Lord taught, and Muhammad began his night-journey to Heaven. This one spot, the Temple Mount or Mount Moriah or the Haram al-Sharif as it is variously called, epitomizes the whole problem of Palestine and of the Holy Places. It is sacred to Jews because it occupies a central place in

Jewish religious tradition and because it is the site of the Wailing Wall (actually the outer wall of the Muslim Haram al-Sharif or Noble Sanctuary). To Christians, there is no other spot so closely associated with the life of Jesus, from childhood to death. And to Muslims, the site of Muhammad's ascent into Heaven is so sacred that they consider Jerusalem to be their third holiest city, after Mecca and Medina.

From our Bible and from our general Western background it is not difficult for us to understand the attachment of Christianity or Judaism to Jerusalem. We are familiar with the story of the early Hebrew prophets, the kings, the Babylonian exile and the return, and finally the dispersion of the Jews when their Temple was razed by the Romans, and we know that ever since Jews all over the world have repeated the prayer "next year in Jerusalem." We also know the associations that the city has for Christians: from the early days of Our Lord's teaching in the Temple, to the events of the Passion, Crucifixion, Resurrection and Ascension. The connection of the Muslims with Jerusalem, however, may require a word of explanation.

Islam, like Judaism and Christianity, with both of which it shares a common background, is a religion of the Book, and the Quran contains considerable material from the Bible. Many Old Testament figures familiar to us reappear in Islamic tradition, beginning with Abraham and going on through Moses, David and Solomon, to name only a few. While we may think of Abraham as the father of the Jews, because of the promises he made to Isaac, his son by Sarah, he is also regarded as the father of the Arabs because of other, and earlier promises he made to his firstborn, Ishmael (son of Hagar) from whom the Arabs claim descent and to whom they refer as Ismail. The concept of a single God, reiterated by the pious Muslim in his prayers five times a day, is basic to Islam, as it is to Judaism and Christianity. So it is understandable that any faith based on this fundamental concept and designed to appeal to seventh century desert folk, largely animist by tradition, should have been rooted in the place where the concept itself originated. Thus it was that Muhammad started his journey up to Heaven from the very spot where the earliest direct confrontation between God and man is said to have taken place: the rock, in Jerusalem, where Abraham went to sacrifice Isaac. And it is equally understandable that when the Arabs conquered Jerusalem they should have built their great shrine on this same site. Over the years this became a place of pilgrimage for Muslims from all over the world. In fact, before the June War, several hundred thousand of them came to Jerusalem not only from neighboring Arab states and Turkey but from as far away as Morocco or Indonesia. It was part of the pilgrimage of a lifetime demanded of the true believer, one of the five requirements of a theologically simple religion.

Thus again we can understand why it was that Muhammad in the early years of his teaching, before the great shrine at Mecca had been built, told his followers to face Jerusalem when they prayed—just as Jewish synagogues all over the world are built to face toward the Holy City, as are many Christian churches. In brief, to discount the Muslim connection with Jerusalem would be as mistaken as to disregard the Christian association with Judaic tradition.

While the Temple area illustrates in the most dramatic fashion the way in which the interests of the three religions are intermingled in the Jerusalem area, the shrines of the three are scattered throughout the Holy City in such a way as to make their physical separation an impossibility. It is this that has caused the rivalries that over the years have made of Jerusalem, and indeed all of Palestine, a scene of conflict.

For us, it was thrilling to live and move where Christ had walked, and as always we found the Bible to be the best guidebook to the Holy Land. To see and to know such spots as the Mount of Olives, the Garden of Gethsemane, or the site of the Last Supper, was a rewarding experience indeed, although to our Western eye the shrines were tawdry and cluttered inside: it was outside, on the hills ringing the City, that we felt closest to the scenes of the Bible, and these associations grew more vivid the longer we stayed on.

It was always a source of keen satisfaction to take our visitors up to the Mount of Olives, itself the scene of so many associations with Jesus, and to look out over the city to the various places featured in the life of Our Lord. As we stood on the very top of the Mount, at the reputed site of the Ascension, we could look straight across the narrow Kidron valley to the Walled City, and its different sites mentioned in the Gospels, from the Temple area to the site of the Crucifixion. Directly across from us was the Golden Gate, said to have been the gate by which Christ entered the city, and walled up for centuries because of a Muslim belief that this would prevent a new Messiah from entering and taking the city.

Frequently we would also take our visitors to the Convent of the Sisters of Zion, inside the Walled City on the Via Dolorosa, the Way of the Cross. First we would go down to the crypt of the building to see the huge Herodian paving stones, deeply scarred by Roman chariot wheels and scratched with the patterns of Roman soldiers' games. Here Jesus is thought to have stood trial before Pilate, for this is the site of the palace-fortress called the Antonia. Then we would climb to the roof of the convent and gaze again out over the city, with its many places evocative of Our Lord.

Historically, Jerusalem has associations running back 4,000 years, and a long record of conquest: the city has been captured some twenty-five times. Around the year 1,000 B. C. David took the city and made it the capital of his kingdom. It continued in Jewish possession until the Babylonian captivity in 587 B. C., and following the return from exile some fifty years later of a small fraction of their number, was held intermittently by the Jews during the next few centuries. These years were marked by one foreign conquest after another, until the Romans took the city in 63 B. C. It was the Roman Emperor Titus in 70 A. D. who destroyed the second Temple and drove out the Jews. By the fourth century of our era, Jerusalem had become a Byzantine city and a place of Christian pilgrimage, as it has been ever since (we know just how the city looked from the sixth century mosaic map uncovered at Madaba in Jordan). The Muslims arrived on the scene in the seventh century, when the city was taken by the Arab armies of the Caliph Umar. For nearly a hundred years, from 1099 to 1187, the Crusaders made it the capital of their Latin Kingdom of Jerusalem. Following the Crusades, the city was held by the Ayyubids, by the Mamelukes of Egypt and, beginning in 1517, by the Ottoman Turks, whose rule lasted just 400 years, until the British under General Allenby entered the city in 1917. After the First World War Jerusalem was the seat of the Mandate for Palestine, administered by the British government. In 1948, upon termination of the Mandate, the city became the scene of heavy fighting and was divided between Israel and Jordan—a situation that lasted until the June War.

Turning now to a description of the city as we knew it in its divided state during the period leading up to the June War, I would think it logical to start with the Walled City (see map 3). This symbolizes Jerusalem to most people and in fact was all there was to the city until about 1860, when the first settlement was made outside the walls. The Walled City, which is one of the best-preserved medieval walled cities in the world, contains most of the important Holy Places in Jerusalem. It is entirely surrounded by a handsome crenellated wall of the tawny local stone, built by the Ottoman Emperor Suleiman the Magnificent in about 1540, and embodying the most beautiful workmanship. It is essential to keep the date of the present walls in mind and to realize that the walls we see today are not those that existed in either Old Testament or New Testament times, although at some points they coincide with the ancient walls. Thus we might be puzzled to find the Church of the Holy Sepulchre, built over what is generally accepted as the site of the Crucifixion and Burial of Christ, to be inside the Walled City, when the Gospel tells us that this event took place outside the city walls—until we learn that the British archaeologist Kathleen Kenyon a few years ago found traces of the contemporary city walls that confirm the Biblical account.

The visitor may also find it disconcerting to see that David's city, the first Jewish city, lies outside the present wall. This site, likewise, known as Mount Ophel, has been confirmed by the archaeologists. It was evidently chosen because it contained the only natural source of water in the entire area (the so-called Virgin's Spring) and because it lay just above the confluence of the two principal valleys in the Jerusalem region, the Kidron and the Hinnom, and could thus be more easily defended.

The Walled City, encompassing an area of approximately one square kilometer with a resident population of about 25,000, was a highly picturesque town within a town, with its teeming bazaars and busy shops. Often we had practically to elbow our way through the crowded cobblestoned byways, always on foot, since few streets are wide enough even for a jeep to pass. Frequently we were jostled by donkeys carrying fruit or vegetables for sale. The shops lining the streets were open stalls, closed by shutters at night and grouped together according to the wares they sold, such as fine European textiles or local cottons and silks, shoes from Rome or Damascus, local copper work, gold jewelry, clothing from almost any country one can think of, and gadgets from Red China, Japan or the USA. The light is dim as the sun filters through the high vaulted roofs of ancient *khans* or caravanserais, with their dark mysterious alcoves, and is not much brighter in the narrow passages between the newer buildings. Many of the older buildings have dome-like roofs of a characteristic Arab construction of mud and plaster, since beams of the size necessary for the roof were lacking at the time they were built. These domes that dot the city skyline are one of the charming details of the view of the rooftops—and they also provide a home-made variety of air conditioning.

The air was full of the cries of street vendors urging the passers-by in Arabic, English or French to inspect their wares, the ever-present radio speakers, the church bells, and the muezzin, calling the faithful to prayer from his minaret (though this call is nowadays almost always a recording). The smells of the bazaars are exotic and tantalizing, varying from one section to another. The pungency of the spices and the rich aroma of the street of the coffee merchants linger in our memory. The unpleasant odors associated with many dark corners were there, too, but far less penetrating than one would expect. As a matter of fact, the Old City throughout was cleaner than the New.

The streets of the Walled City, and indeed of the whole Arab city, presented a fascinating and continuous parade of humanity, from the soldiers in their *kaffiyahs* or Arab headgear, to the many Catholic priests, white-robed or black or wearing the brown habit of the Franciscans, the Orthodox priests with their beards and tall, brimless hats (*kalimoukion*), the Muslim *mullahs* in their brown or black robes, and the lines of school children in uniform. The most colorful touch came from the village women in their traditional dresses, elaborately embroidered in ancient patterns, which varied in color and motif from one town to another. However, practically all the residents of the Old City wore normal Western dress, the women devoting much care and attention to their chic but conservative appearance. Veiled women are practically never seen in the city and among the men the *tarbush* (fez) is rare. On the other hand, the *kaffiyah*, a red and white or black and white checked kerchief type of head-dress, is quite common among the men, and increasingly so as a means of identification since the Israeli occupation. This is probably the most dashing headgear in the world when worn by one born to it; the trailing ends can be wrapped around the neck to keep out the wind and rain, they can be tossed over one ear or the other to give shade from the sun or one-sided protection as the weather may require, or, on a fine spring day, when the mood is gay, both ends will be tossed up over the head and down the back. Only an Arab can do this with just the right flair.

Everywhere were the tourists and pilgrims, to many of whom a visit to the Holy City was the fulfillment of a lifetime ambition. Each year some 500,000 to 600,000 visitors came to the Old City and thronged the streets at the times of their respective Christian or Muslim feasts— the Muslims on their way to or from the *Hajj* (the pilgrimage to Mecca). The importance of tourism to the economy of Jerusalem, and of Jordan, is not always appreciated. It was estimated that 75 per cent of the tourists arriving in Jordan entered *via* Jerusalem airport, and that the country's income from tourism was between $30,000,000 and $40,000,000 per year, well over half of it being accounted for by the Old City. Many residents of the city—hotel keepers and their employees, guides, tourist agents, taxi drivers, bus drivers, dealers in curios and antiquities, and the like—were dependent for their livelihood on the tourist trade, which since the June War has declined to what is at best a subsistence level.

The inner city is divided into four quarters: Christian, Armenian, Jewish and Muslim. The Jewish Quarter, running up to the Wailing Wall at the edge of the Muslim Quarter, formerly contained a number of synagogues, but many of the buildings were destroyed during the fierce fighting which preceded the evacuation of the area by Jewish forces in 1948 or had fallen into disrepair since then. For the next nineteen years, the Jewish Quarter remained more or less of a ruin, populated only by a few Arab refugees and other poor people.

Aside from the Wailing Wall, the principal shrines in the Walled City are the Church of the Holy Sepulchre and the Haram al-Sharif, in the Christian and Muslim Quarters, respectively.

The Church of the Holy Sepulchre, which, with the Church of the Nativity at Bethlehem, is a leading site of Christian pilgrimage, covers under one roof the reputed location of Calvary and the Tomb of Our Lord. There has been a church here since the fourth century, when the Emperor Constantine erected a large circular church, of which traces can still be seen. It was Constantine's mother, the Empress Helena, who came to Jerusalem toward the end of the third century with the aim of locating the principal sites connected with Christ. In fact, most of the Christian sites venerated as such today were identified by Helena at that time. In the case of the Holy Sepulchre, her task was facilitated by the fact that it was known that the Roman Emperior Hadrian in the second century had built a temple to Venus on the site of Calvary, in an attempt to obliterate all Christian associations, and the temple was still standing when she arrived on the scene.

There have been several reconstructions of the church since Constantine's time though basically the building today is as the Crusaders rebuilt it in the twelfth century: the façade, for example, incorporates some superb Romanesque stone carving. The church is always full of visitors. Many people find the crowds, the multiplicity of shrines and the profusion of clerics, with each sect claiming a different part of the building, to be confusing if not downright distasteful. One has to visit the church many times before its real quality as one of the main shrines of the Christian faith begins to emerge. As a result of the skillful reconstruction now going on, the church is beginning to achieve an architectural unity it has not had for a long time, as more and more of the ugly partitions cutting up the interior are removed.

Many of the more pious pilgrims approach the Holy Sepulchre along the Via Dolorosa, laid out in the fourteenth century as symbolic of the route Jesus could have followed on his way to the Crucifixion. Every Friday there is a procession which anyone can join and follow the route, with pauses for prayer at the fourteen Stations of the Cross along the way.

The other great monument of the Walled City is the enclosure called the Haram al-Sharif. The principal structure in the Haram is the Dome of the Rock, which stands at the highest point of the enclosure and which is presumed to be on the site of the Jewish Temple. Directly beneath is the rock associated with Abraham and Muhammad. The Dome of the Rock is an exquisite shrine, erected in the late seventh century in the same architectural pattern as that of the Eastern churches of the time, the circular form seen from Constantinople to Rome and Ravenna and Aix-la-Chapelle. It is essentially a more modern and perhaps more refined version of the Church of the Holy Sepulchre as built by Constantine three centuries earlier. The dome is supported on a circle of immense columns, the inner ring of a double-vaulted ambulatory. The interior walls are covered with mosaics reflecting the many artistic influences adapted by the Arabs, while the exterior is marked by a dome of bright gold, with brilliant tiles on the walls in the Persian manner. The building stands today as perfectly proportioned as when it was first constructed. The Crusaders used it as a church and called it the *Templum Domini* or Temple of the Lord. The knights who administered it were known as the Knights Templar and the building served as a model for the Temple Church in London. With the neighboring Al-Aqsa Mosque, silver domed and dating from the early eighth century, the Dome of the Rock serves to make the entire Haram area a place of great beauty and dignity which fully lives up to its name of Noble Sanctuary.

Outside the Walled City, it would seem natural to continue with a description of the Jordanian sector of Jerusalem since it surrounded the inner city to the north, east and south. It is only toward the west that the city wall touched on the non-man's land separating the two sectors. Immediately to the east is the Kidron valley and beyond it the Garden of Gethsemane, on the lower slope of the Mount of Olives. In the valley and stretching up the Mount are many Jewish tombs, placed here because of their nearness to the Temple and because of an ancient tradition that on the Day of Judgment these tombs will be the first to be opened. The Garden of Gethsemane, with its ancient, gnarled olive trees, some of which look as though they were surely in existence in Our Lord's day, always seemed to be one of the most satisfying of the sacred sites in Jerusalem, not only for the beauty of its setting but also because it is an oasis of peace and quiet away from the noise and bustle of the city. The Mount of Olives was also a favorite spot, both because of the incomparable views it affords and because of its New Testament associations.

The Mount of Olives is a good place from which to get an idea not only of the city but also of the hills ringing Jerusalem, starting with the Mount of Evil Counsel to the south (so-called because of Judas Iscariot's betrayal of Jesus), and the site in recent years of United Nations Headquarters, and next the Mount of Offense (a reference to the fact that King Solomon had certain non-Jewish wives who had to be housed outside the city), Mount Ophel, Mount Zion and Mount Moriah in the immediate vicinity of the Walled City, Mount Scopus which is really a continuation of the Mount of Olives, and in the distance to the north, the hill called Nabi Samwil, meaning the prophet Samuel in Arabic. This was the *Mons Gaudii* (Hill of Joy) of the Crusaders because it was from there that many of them first glimpsed the Holy City.

Mount Scopus was another place from which the Holy City was often first viewed and its name, from the Latin, reflects this fact, as does its Hebrew name, *Har Hatsofim* or the Mount of Observation. It is the highest hill in the Jerusalem area and, like the Mount of Olives, commands a splendid view not only toward the city but also to the east, past the arid, rocky desert (the wilderness of Zin of the Bible) to the Dead Sea and beyond, in trans-Jordan, the Mountains of Moab. The descent to the Dead Sea takes one down some 4,000 feet from Jerusalem, as the city is 2,500 feet above and the sea 1,500 feet below the level of the Mediterranean. The Dead Sea is, in fact, the lowest spot on earth. In winter many residents of the Old City maintained weekend cottages at Jericho in the Jordan valley just above the Dead Sea, and a hotel, casino, and even horse racing of sorts flourished by the shores of the sea.

Mount Scopus was the site of the original Hebrew University and Hadassah Hospital, both built during the early years of the British Mandate. At the end of the fighting in 1948 an agreement was made between the Arab and Jewish commanders whereby these two institutions were placed in a special enclave to which the Israelis were permitted to have access periodically through the Arab territory which surrounded it on every side. They were allowed to maintain a police guard at the two buildings and rotate it every two weeks, under the supervision of the United Nations. We often saw the biweekly convoy assemble for this purpose and proceed, with its UN and

Jordanian Army escort, through a portion of the Jordanian sector and back, a distance of perhaps a mile. The hospital and university buildings were maintained primarily for prestige purposes and as military strongpoints. By 1967 they had fallen into a very considerable state of disrepair.

Near the Scopus enclave, and separated from it by a strip of no-man's land, is the Augusta Victoria Hospital, a large baronial structure erected early in this century with funds provided by Kaiser Wilhelm of Germany and thought by some, owing to its dominating position on the hilltop and its elaborate decoration, to have been intended by him to be the seat of an eventual German colonial administration. In the early days of the Mandate it was used by the British High Commissioners and more recently served as a hospital for Arab refugees, administered by the Lutheran World Federation for the UN.

The area immediately to the north of the Walled City contains the modern commercial center of the Jordanian city and here are located many hotels and travel agencies. Here also is the Palestine Archaeological Museum (sometimes called the Rockefeller Museum since that family had originally endowed it), housing an impressive collection of antiquities from excavations all over Palestine, antedating 1948, and the extensive collection of Dead Sea Scrolls, still being pieced together and prepared for publication by scholars from all over the world under the direction of Père Roland de Vaux of the *Ecole Biblique* in the Old City. It was always a fascinating experience to go with the curator, Dr. Yusuf Saad, into the work rooms and see how the Scrolls were studied and photographed by the infra-red process. Nearby were the original benches and implements discovered at Qumran near the Dead Sea, where the Scrolls were discovered. In its entirety we found this exhibition of the Scrolls to be more interesting than the much more elegantly displayed one at the Israel Museum in the New City.

It was unfortunate, as events showed, that in 1966 the Jordanian government had seen fit to nationalize the museum and take it out of the hands of the international board that had administered it since Mandate times. This made it an easy matter for the Israelis, after the June War, to take it over as enemy property. Since the war, incidentally, the Dead Sea Scrolls exhibition there has been closed.

To the north of the Walled City, and to a lesser extent to the east and south, there has been considerable development in recent years, as the residents of the New City discovered to their surprise when they came back to the Old City after the June War. Virtually the entire area as far as Kalandia airport, some six miles north, is built up. It con-

Upsala College
Library
East Orange, N. J.

tains many substantial stone houses, with surrounding gardens, giving proof of the prosperity which had come to the city, partly as a result of US aid, but mainly from the expansion of tourism. A master plan for the city, developed by the British town planner Henry Kendall in late Mandate times and revised by him in more recent years, was being put into operation and there was much building activity throughout the area of the outer city. There was also much general economic activity as a result of the position of the Old City as the commercial hub of the entire West Bank of the Jordan.

Passing from the Jordanian to the Israeli sector at Mandelbaum Gate, just beyond our Old City Consulate, we would cross the no-man's land, with its ruined, roofless buildings dating from the 1948 war, the ground overgrown with weeds, a scene of utter desolation. The area on either side of us, we were warned, was thickly sown with mines—indeed, we knew of one Jordanian soldier who had had his leg blown off when he trod in the wrong place. We could see that many houses adjoining the no-man's land on either side had been converted into military strongpoints through the use of concrete and barbed wire. Shots were often exchanged from one side to the other in moments of tension.

By way of contrast with Israel's other cities, Tel Aviv and Haifa, which are primarily industrial and commercial in character, the New City is more of an intellectual and religious center. Indeed, as soon as we passed Mandelbaum Gate we came to the Orthodox quarter of Mea Shearim (meaning a hundred gates), the streets of which provided a picturesque sight, the men with their beards and ringlets, fur hats and prayer shawls and the women with their billowing skirts and bonnets covering shaved heads. Aside from the Orthodox element, the people of the city dress in the European style, though with considerable emphasis on shorts for both men and women and with many men sporting the typically Israeli open necked shirt (it was said that when David Ben Gurion was Prime Minister he would not allow anyone to attend Cabinet meetings wearing a tie). The wearing by women of short shorts, miniskirts and tight-fitting slacks is quite common, in sharp contrast to the conservative way in which the women of the Arab sector dress.

Beyond the Orthodox quarter lies the commercial center, with the streets always crowded and noisy (there are even traffic lights, which do not exist in the Old City). Here are the hotels, the cinemas, the shops, and, across the street from a park which had formerly been a Muslim cemetery our New City Consulate General. On a hill stands the King David Hotel, the best known hotel of the city in British days, commanding a fine view of the Old City walls, a short distance to the east—but a whole world away. The King David is always full of tourists, the great majority of them Jewish and many of them American. Across the street is the YMCA, an imposing edifice erected through the generosity of an American millionaire in the 1930s and offering the only complete recreational facilities for men, women and children in the city, with a membership of 3,800 (of whom 95 per cent are Jewish—one of the largest "Y" memberships in the world).

From the King David and the YMCA one could look across eastward to Mount Zion, located near the southwest corner of the city wall but on the Israeli side, containing the so-called Tomb of David and the Room of the Last Supper, another of the sites identified by the Empress Helena, although some scholars now think Mount Zion should really be regarded as being Mount Moriah. Going west one comes next to the older residential quarters of Rehavia and Talbieh, with tree shaded streets and an air of considerable distinction, and then the newer portions of the city. Because the narrow Jerusalem corridor, linking the city to the rest of Israel and secured after bitter fighting in the 1948 war, was a salient thrusting eastwards into Jordanian territory, any extension of the city after 1948 had to take place to the west. Here, on a series of hills, are the new government offices, the Israel Museum, the Knesset (Parliament) building, the convention hall where we attended the concerts of the Israel Philharmonic Orchestra, the new Hebrew University, and on the outskirts of the city, the new Hadassah Hospital. Much of this new construction is of reinforced concrete, which does not have the charm of the characteristic honey-colored Jerusalem stone.

The relocation of Hadassah and the University in their handsome and impressive new quarters in the western part of the city, and the construction of the Israel Museum, which opened its doors in May of 1965, were accomplished with primarily American financial assistance. We came to know all three institutions well, and many of our closest Israeli friends were connected with them.

Jerusalem is probably the only city in the world with a brand new university center which started completely from scratch and, thanks to foreign generosity, emerged fully built and equipped within the space of only a few years. The University, which prides itself on being the university not just of Israel but of the whole Jewish people, is the center of the intellectual life of the city. Included among its 11,000 to 12,000 students were about 500 Americans and some 200 to 400 Israeli

Arabs. With a few exceptions, instruction at the University is in the Hebrew language, which means that the American and other foreign students (many of whom are Africans) have to take a special intensive course in Hebrew before beginning their classes. It also limited the number of Arabs who could qualify for admission. Affiliated with the University is the National Library, a large collection which is one of the finest in the Middle East.

Hadassah, located on a commanding height overlooking the village of Ain Karim, traditionally regarded as the birthplace of John the Baptist, is famous for its synagogue with stained glass windows by Marc Chagall depicting the twelve tribes of Israel. The hospital prides itself on its modern equipment, much of it provided from the United States by Hadassah, the Women's Zionist Organization of America.

The Israel Museum was built to combine four collections: the former fine arts and archaeological museums, the Dead Sea Scrolls and the Billy Rose Sculpture Garden. The buildings are handsome and the exhibits, which as might be expected include many items of Jewish historical interest such as an entire eighteenth century synagogue from northern Italy, are well mounted. Often at night the Museum buildings and the Crusader Monastery of the Cross next door would be floodlit in a most spectacular way: the Monastery, incidentally, is said to have been built on the site of the tree from which Our Lord's Cross was fashioned.

In the western parts of the city is much of the housing constructed in haste and at minimum cost in the years immediately following independence in order to accommodate the many new immigrants who came in during this period. This housing consists of stark, modern apartment buildings which are hardly pleasing to the eye but which serve a utilitarian purpose. Construction of this sort is still going on.

From almost any point in the New City it was possible to see the Jordanian territory which surrounded the city on three sides. Beyond Hadassah Hospital the hills begin to run downwards to the coastal plain, a descent not as abrupt as that toward the Dead Sea on the other side and with considerably more vegetation, both because the rainfall is much greater on the western slopes and because of determined efforts over the years at reforestation.

So much for the physical aspect of Jerusalem as we knew it. The contrasts between the two parts of the city were marked, but it would be an oversimplification to define them simply in terms of ancient versus modern, or old versus new. It is true that the general appearance of the New City was more modern than that of the Old. This was due partly to the fact that the portions of the city which the Israelis inherited in 1948 were on the whole the newer and more developed areas, and partly to the fact that since then many of the fine old stone houses so typical of Jerusalem had been torn down and replaced by modern concrete buildings as a part of the Israeli development of the city.

It is also true that there was a difference in the things we were apt to take our visitors to see in the two sectors: in the New City it would be the superb new buildings of the University, the Museum, or Hadassah Hospital, while in the Old City it would be the monuments of the past and especially the Walled City, virtually unchanged for centuries. At the same time, in recent years there had been a very considerable development of the Old City, especially in the business district just north of the Walled City in the neighborhood of Salah al-din Street and in the area leading out to the airport. It was therefore not only a matter of comparing new and old.

A more meaningful way of contrasting the two sectors would be to say that the general cultural orientation of the New City was Western and that of the Old City Eastern. Thus Israel offered more intellectual stimulus, more cultural attractions such as concerts or art exhibitions, than did Jordan. In the New City, there was the world-famous symphony orchestra, which attracted guest conductors and soloists from all over, but there was nothing comparable in the Old City. As one walked along the streets of the Israeli city one frequently noted art galleries and there was a flourishing artists' colony made up of local people, centering in the Artists' House. Here again there was nothing comparable on the Jordanian side. I would attribute this situation largely to a lingering cultural isolation on the part of the Arabs, going back to their generally backward condition during 400 years of Turkish rule, followed by the period of the Mandate, when their cultural development was virtually neglected as compared with the Jews of Palestine, who brought in a constant infusion of Western ideas. The result was that the intellectual life of the Old City as we knew it tended still to be dominated by its foreign residents. This does not mean, however, that our Old City friends did not welcome such cultural attractions as came to the city or that there were no active local artists or musicians. It is merely that there was a marked contrast with the Israeli side, due to an obvious lack of foreign support.

The differing cultural orientation of the two sectors showed itself in other ways. Israel was dynamic: life was real and hard and earnest and there were very few frills. In Jordan, a more leisurely pace was apparent. People took time to sit down at the coffee house and exchange news. In Israel, people drank coffee too, but often on the run, standing at a counter. The traffic in the New City seemed to move at a faster clip and altogether there was more bustle and activity, more sense of a mission to be accomplished and a nation being built in a hurry.

In a different vein, a feature of the New City that had no counterpart across the Armistice line was the all-pervasive influence of the Orthodox Jews. The Sabbath, beginning before sunset on Friday and running until after sundown on Saturday, was rigidly enforced. No buses or regular taxis ran, cinemas and other places of amusement were closed and Jerusalem became a dead city (we had to send our Israeli employees home early on Friday afternoons, so they could get there before the buses stopped and cook their food for the next 24 hours). There was practically no traffic in the streets aside from the cars of foreigners and sometimes these would be stoned on passing near the Orthodox quarter.

There was nothing comparable to the Jewish Sabbath on the Jordanian side: true, government offices were closed on Friday, the Muslim day of rest, and so were some Muslim shops. On Sunday a few Christian shops were closed but it was often a case of personal choice as to "business as usual" on both days. Indeed, life picked up on weekends and this resulted after the June War in an influx of unrestrained non-observant Jews into the Old City on Fridays and Saturdays.

Another influence in the New City which permeated every aspect of its life was that of the Holocaust, the slaughter of five to six million Jews in Hitler's Europe. No friend of ours had escaped the loss of a relative—some indeed had lost their entire families—and the press daily kept these memories alive. These two influences combined to make nearly every occasion of national commemoration a solemn one.

Another dominant aspect of life in the New City was its austerity. This could readily be seen by comparing the shops and markets of the two halves of the city. Israel's economy was a spartan one with respect to imported goods and these, particularly luxury items, were hard to come by. In the shops, stocks were smaller than in the Old City and there was much less selection. Nearly everything in the way of food, clothing and articles for the household was of Israeli origin and many of the manufactured articles were cheaply made. In addition, prices were high. Fortunately we could do our shopping on both sides and thus benefit from the greater profusion of imported goods of all kinds in the Old City. Private American citizens, however, who were temporary residents of the New City, often complained to us of the quantity as well as the quality of what was available—meat, for example—and the prices they had to pay. They also had difficulty in locating suitably furnished housing, in keeping warm in winter, in finding schooling for their children (if they did not happen to know Hebrew) and in finding domestic help, even part time. In all of these respects, the Jordanian sector was an easier place for a foreigner to live.

Another difference between the two parts of the city lay in the fact that Israel is a welfare state, with elaborate social services for the entire population. From the beginning there was a highly developed trade union structure and wages and hours of work were closely regulated, as any employer of labor can testify. Jordan was less advanced with regard to matters of this sort, although there were some fairly well developed welfare services and some rudimentary trade unions. The army hospitals, which took care of all the members of a soldier's family, were well equipped and furnished perhaps the closest equivalent to the socialized medicine provided in Israel.

A final and fundamental point that I would like to make with respect to the Jerusalem we knew before the June War is that while for nineteen years it seemed two different cities—even two different worlds—paradoxically it was essentially one city. It was only those of us who went back and forth constantly from one side to the other who could grasp its essential oneness, especially if we had known the city before. The residents of each sector, and the tourists who crossed in one direction only, saw the city as basically a divided one. For my part, in spite of the barbed wire and the barricades and the many contrasts between the sectors, I am convinced that the partition of Jerusalem, a partition that was certainly most deplorable, existed not so much on the ground as in the minds of men. And so it is to the people of the divided city and their attitudes toward each other that we now turn our attention.

III

The People

Just as the Jerusalem we knew before the June War was divided into two halves, so was our acquaintanceship; in fact, one might say, that like Gaul, it fell into three parts, since in addition to the Arab and Jewish residents of the city there were the internationals, the foreigners who had been attracted there by the special status of Jerusalem as an international and, especially, a religious center. Before coming to this last group, however, I will give an account of our Jewish and Arab contacts and attempt some comparisons between the two cultures that they represented, since it is an underlying theme of this book that the partition was essentially in the minds of men. It is in this last direction that some fundamental changes must be made if there is to be peace in the Holy Land.

Taking first our New City friends, I would say that the thing that differentiated them from our Old City friends was that they were basically Western in their orientation. I am speaking here of the Jewish residents of the city whom we knew: the local government officials and persons connected with Hebrew University, Hadassah Hospital and the business and intellectual life of the city who made up our circle of acquaintances and friends.

During much of our stay in Jerusalem the Mayor of the Israeli sector was the ebullient Teddy Kollek, who was to be proclaimed Mayor of all Jerusalem after the June War and who was the chief architect of the policy of "Greater Jerusalem," that is, the integration of the Old City with the New. Prior to his becoming Mayor, we had already come to know Teddy (as everyone called him) as the organizing force behind the new Israel Museum and as an ardent collector of antiquities. He was both a stimulating companion as well as one of the leaders of modern Israel. Short, stocky, with shirt open at the neck and the general air of a suppressed dynamo, he went about his duties

28

with zeal and gusto—and the municipal problems with which he had to cope were complex and frustrating, even before the war. We heard after the war that during the forty-eight hours the New City was under shellfire, he was constantly on the go, driving all over town in his well-worn car, seeing to the safety and welfare of his fellow townspeople, with a complete disregard for his own skin. In many ways Kollek typified to us the dynamic, vital character of Israeli society.

Our oldest Israeli friends were the President of the Hebrew University, Eliahu Elath, and his wife Zehava. We had known them in Washington and London, in both of which he had served as Ambassador, and they were unfailingly kind to us, giving help and advice of all sorts and putting us into contact with a host of interesting people. Elath is a distinguished Orientalist and a graduate of the American University of Beirut. He and his wife, an accomplished sculptress, are prominent among the citizens of Jerusalem and we always enjoyed our visits to their home. Speaking both Arabic and Persian, he had many contacts in the neighboring countries prior to 1948 and in the many talks we had regarding the current Middle Eastern scene his attitude was one of unfailing wisdom and compassion.

Another University couple with whom we were friendly were the Even-Aris. Professor Michael Even-Ari, like many Israelis, has changed his name to the Hebrew form, in this case the equivalent of his original Leowenstein, or Lion's Stone, *Even* meaning "stone" and *Ari* "lion." He is a renowned botanist and agricultural expert. He runs an experimental station in the arid south of the country, the Negev, where he has developed new techniques of dry farming, using only the water accumulated in gullies by national drainage after the fashion of the ancient Nabatean inhabitants of the region. These techniques have been adopted by several foreign countries, an example of Israeli technical cooperation abroad. Mrs. Even-Ari is likewise a botanist and my wife often went to her for advice about the flowers in the Consulate garden.

At the University we also enjoyed knowing the Librarian, Dr. Curt Wormann, and his assistant who ran the music section, Dr. Israel Adler. One of our most interesting mornings in Jerusalem was spent with them at the Library, examining their collection of old books and manuscripts and then looking in at the music library where a group of technicians was engaged in making tape recordings of Oriental music, in this case Kurdish. The fact that these Israeli scholars were making a study of this sort made us wonder whether the Arabs were undertaking a similarly deep inquiry into Israeli culture. We thought this to be obviously unlikely.

The grand old lady of the city was Mrs. Beatrice Magnes (recently deceased) from New York, the widow of Dr. Judah Magnes, an American Jew who had been the first President of the Hebrew University. Dr. Magnes was one of the founders of the *Ihud* (Union) movement, which had as its objective the encouragement of Arab-Jewish cooperation. I recall that his testimony made a powerful impression on the Anglo-American Committee of Inquiry, with which I spent some time in the Jerusalem of 1946. (The *Ihud* movement still exists in Israel although the climate for cooperation between Arabs and Jews has hardly been auspicious in recent years.)

The Magnes' son, Jonathan, is a professor of physiology at the Hebrew University. His charming wife, Hava, originally from Vienna, is a leader in the National Council of Jewish Women and was the driving force behind the building of the new YMHA.

Jerusalem is the center for much of Israel's modern painting and sculpture. Artists' House was organized and opened during our stay and the dynamic young Mrs. Etienne Debell who runs it is doing a splendid job of bringing together young artists in the congenial atmosphere of an old Arab house. We attended many exhibitions there and were also welcomed at the studios of several of the established Israeli artists. Among these were Isador Aschheim, two of whose paintings we brought back to the United States with us; Reuben Reuven, Ludwig Blum and Mrs. Anna Ticho, as well as the sculptor David Palombo, who had his studio in a restored Turkish caravansarai on Mount Zion. He was tragically killed in an accident during our stay in the city. We have one of his works, too, a small bronze in the rugged style he employed with such success in his great bronze gates for the new Parliament building and for the Yad Vashem, the shrine of remembrance for the victims of the Holocaust.

The cultural attractions of the New City included not only the art exhibitions and the Israel Museum but most importantly the Israel Philharmonic Orchestra. Through the intervention of friends, for there is always a packed house, we managed to secure season tickets to the concerts, and the evenings we spent there, surrounded by friends and exhilarated by the wonderful music, are among our most precious memories. The concerts were easily the foremost artistic and social events of the year. Frequently there would be visiting performers, such as the musicians from Marlboro under the direction of Rudolf

Serkin, or the New York City Ballet, to name two groups which came out under US government auspices.

We never ceased to be astonished at the variety of national origins of our Israeli acquaintances. Among those I have mentioned, Elath is from Russia, Wormann was German by birth and Adler French. Kollek was born in Vienna and Even-Ari in Metz. But in addition, we knew two Scottish couples at Hadassah and two Irish Jews from Dublin. Other friends were South African, Polish, English and, of course, American, in origin. A Canadian doctor at Hadassah had a lovely wife from Vienna and a lawyer from one of the old Jerusalem families had a very chic wife from Alexandria, Egypt. It is said that Israel's population comes from at least seventy-five different countries. It is not uncommon to walk down the street and see blond or red-headed Israelis, and certainly it cannot be said that there is such a thing as a single Israeli racial type.

Finally, I would like to make some mention of our friends from among the old Sephardi families established in Jerusalem for centuries, who spoke Arabic and had had many Arab friends in the old days: the Yeshayas, Eliachars, Astrucs and others. This element in Jerusalem's society could be called more moderate in its outlook toward the neighboring Arab world than the Israelis of European origin. After the war they were glad to resume contact with friends from the Old City and in the future it is to be hoped that they may play a significant rôle in bringing the two communities together.

Although the influence of Orthodoxy was strong in the New City, most of our friends either were non-observing or were Conservative Jews. We were thus not brought into close contact with the Orthodox element in the city's population. These tended in any case to keep to themselves, in Mea Shearim and adjoining quarters of town. Some of the Orthodox harbored extreme political views and had never accepted the idea of a Jewish state (they considered that it should come from God, not from man); a small group, called the Neturei Karta, even refused to recognize the authority of the Israeli government and would not pay taxes or do military service.

The outstanding characteristic of our New City friends was that they were so intellectually stimulating. Entertaining was on a simple scale as none of our friends had regular servants. Dinners were small and relaxed or, as frequently happened, a few friends were simply invited in for coffee and conversation after dinner. These evenings invariably produced the most fascinating sort of talk. We were often the only foreigners present and the conversation would range all over the horizon, from the war in Vietnam to problems of religion or philosophy. We recall especially our visits to the home of the late Haim Krongold, who for many years headed the committee of the Philharmonic Orchestra, and his wife, Rosa. On one occasion they had us to a piano recital by a talented young Israeli couple. On another, we heard an account of Christ's Trial and Crucifixion from the legal point of view, given by a Justice of Israel's Supreme Court. One evening, at the home of a local physician, we listened to three exponents of the chief branches of Jewry—Orthodox, Conservative and Reform—explaining Judaism from their separate viewpoints, in sharp disagreement but always in good humor. These evenings were in great contrast to those we spent in the Jordanian sector, where the chief and generally the only topic of conversation on the part of our Arab friends was the Palestine problem and America's nefarious rôle in the setting up of Israel.

By way of offering a few general characterizations of the Israeli people, based on our acquaintance in the New City and observations running back over the years, I would say that they are a people with tremendous drive, energy and ability, and a complete dedication to the Zionist ideal; tough minded, ruthless, yet with a keen appreciation of the rôle of the arts in life. I often used to think that they had only one blind spot. This was their attitude toward, and lack of understanding of, the Arabs.

The picture I have tried to paint of the people on the Israeli side of the line is necessarily deficient in three main respects. As already explained, we were not in contact with the officials of the central government, by their choice, not ours. It also happened that we had relatively little contact with the Oriental Jews, who now make up more than one-half of Israel's Jewish population. Finally, we did not know very many Israeli Arabs.

The reason for our lack of acquaintance among both Oriental Jews and Israeli Arabs was the same: there were not many of them in Jerusalem. There were of course the long-established Sephardi Jewish families that I have already mentioned. But the vast majority of the Oriental Jews have come to the country since it became independent in 1948 and as a matter of government policy have been accommodated in the new development towns. These have been set up at various localities throughout the countryside in an effort to get people out of the three main cities (Jerusalem, Tel Aviv and Haifa) where more than fifty per cent of Israel's population lives. As for the Arabs, it just happened that there are very few Arab residents of the New City, the overwhelming majority of the Arab population being concentrated in the north (in Galilee) or in the south (in the desert regions). Almost all the Arabs we did know were our own employees. Indeed, about half of the local employees at our New City Consulate were Arabs, who seemed to prefer working for us than for Israeli Jews.

In spite of the fact that our experience of these two groups, the Oriental Jews and the Arabs of Israel, was not as extensive as I would have liked, I think I can safely make the general comment that in present-day Israel the Oriental Jews and the Arabs are very much the "hewers of wood and drawers of water" for the dominant Ashkenazi (European) element and that this will cause social dislocations in the future. The Oriental Jews, coming from the countries of Asia and North Africa, have a completely different outlook from that of the European, socialist-inclined Jews who founded and were for so many years the mainstay of the Zionist movement. The background of the Oriental Jews, in fact, is essentially Arab. Their values are traditionalist, as are those of the Arab world whose language they speak. They tend to be more religious than the Jews of European origin, a fact which accounts in large measure for the influence which Orthodoxy holds in Israel today as compared with the Jewish community in Palestine under the Mandate.

It is true, of course, that all Israeli citizens are equal under the law and that the Hebrew language, which all immigrants of whatever origin must immediately learn, is a great leveler. At the same time, the Oriental Jews simply do not have what it takes to compete with their European brethren on a basis of equality. They have come from very humble surroundings—sometimes literally from caves in the hills, as in Libya. As compared with the European Jews, their families tend to be twice as large, and their family income one-half. Most of them, especially the women, are illiterate when they arrive. In the Oriental community there are more crime and juvenile delinquency than in the European. This community, moreover, has a representation in government, in the professions and in the upper echelons generally far smaller than its relative numbers would indicate. The Oriental Jews complain that actual discrimination is practiced against them by the dominant Western element. Some of the Oriental Jews say openly they want to go home, not having found a welcome in Israel. Certainly there is very little intermarriage between the two groups.

All of these latent causes of friction can be expected to remain in the background so long as Israel's public position is one of being surrounded by hostile neighbors bent on its destruction. This provides an interesting field for speculation if there should ever be a real peace in the area. In any event, it can hardly be said that the egalitarian state dreamed of by the first Zionist planners has come to be.

The situation of the Israeli Arabs is similar in many ways. Prior to the June War they numbered about 250,000 and tended to divide into two main groupings: those who had made their peace with the régime and had decided to cooperate with it; and those who were simply apathetic. It is interesting that three of the four Communist members in the Israeli Parliament are Arabs—this is a way of making a protest. In view of events since 1948, the lot of the Israeli Arab is certainly not a happy one. Inevitably the Arabs are regarded as a fifth column by their Jewish fellow-citizens and inevitably there is discrimination in such things as jobs and housing. Until recently the Arabs were restricted as to where they could live and travel within Israel. These restrictions were in the process of being modified when the June War came. Israeli Arabs cannot serve in the armed forces, which is understandable in view of the likelihood that Israel's wars will be fought with the Arab states, but which serves to set them off from the rest of the population. It is only fair to add that during the crisis leading to the 1967 war, and during the war itself, there were no incidents involving the Israeli Arab population and no problems between the two communities. However, the Arabs remain very much the third class citizens.

A further comment regarding the structure of Israeli society should be made. The social tensions to which I have alluded will be intensified in future because of the fact that the rates of natural increase of the three segments of the population, Ashkenazi Jews, Sephardi Jews and Arabs, are exactly the opposite of the relative positions these elements occupy in the social structure. That is to say the Arabs have the highest rate, the Oriental Jews come next, and the European Jews are last. Indeed, it is said that taking into account the 1,000,000 Arabs now under Israeli control, the Jews will be a minority within 20 years.

The social strains that are latent within Israel should be considered in the light of the fact that Jewish immigration into Israel has diminished very considerably. In 1966 and 1967 net immigration was of the magnitude of not over 20,000 per year, and it is hard to conceive that it will rise greatly in the future. Outside of Israel, the largest Jewish populations today are in the United States and the Soviet bloc and there does not seem to be much prospect of any substantial outflow from either of these sources. The countries of North Africa and Asia which provided almost all of the immigrants in the years since 1948 now have very few Jews left.

Just as the general cultural orientation of our New City friends was Western, that of our Old City friends was Eastern. Our Arab acquaintances in the Old City and throughout the West Bank were Palestinians, who tended to be critical of the central government in Amman and who were obsessed with the Palestine problem. Many of them had had to leave their homes in what became Israel and they remained bitter. This was true both of the Muslims and of the Christians whom we knew. The Christians, who were a much more influential element here than elsewhere in Jordan, had become especially disillusioned with the Amman government. Most of them sent their children abroad for education if they could afford it. Many of these never came back.

In fact, we constantly had the impression that these West Bank Christians feared to speak up against the increasingly militant voices heard from Amman and the other Arab capitals. By sending their children out of the country they gave expression, in virtually the only way possible for them, to their opposition to the growing Muslim control over the schools and to diminishing concern by the government for the needs of the West Bank and the Old City. The exodus, however, was not confined to the children of the people we knew, nor to Christians. During our stay in Jerusalem, there began to take place what amounted to an Arab brain drain. Many of the best educated people, especially teachers, were leaving. Some of them came to our country—ironically enough the relaxation of our immigration quota restrictions at about this time, which most Americans regarded as a progressive move, made this easier. I even had Jordanians complain to me that we were encouraging the exodus in this manner. Others went to the oil producing countries, such as Kuwayt, where they could earn good money and send part of it home to their relatives. It is sad to record that the Jordanian authorities consistently failed to realize the effects of this emigration on the quality of the nation. In fact, the government seems to have focussed its attention more on the volume of the emigrants' remittances, which in 1966 were the equivalent of some $27,000,000 and were thus an important source of foreign exchange for the Kingdom.

Those of our Palestinian friends who had taken refuge in the Old City and elsewhere on the West Bank in 1948 were determined not to go through the experience of fleeing from their homes again, if there should be another war. Repeatedly they would tell us that next time they would stand their ground, come what may. And this is what they did in June 1967; the Arabs who fled to the East Bank of the Jordan during and after the war were almost all refugees from the camps or poor, ignorant people, not the substantial citizens we knew. The attitude of our friends in this respect was essentially one of pride, a typical Arab reaction.

Our contacts in the Jordanian sector were mainly professional people: bankers, lawyers, doctors and the like. As was the case in the New City, we had many friends in the medical profession and it was a pleasure for us to learn, right after the war, that the two groups of doctors had met. Among our Jordanian doctor friends were an internationally known nutrition expert who was doing research on a US government grant, an outstanding brain surgeon, and a prominent chest specialist. Nearly all were connected with Augusta Victoria Hospital and a number of them were fond of outdoor life; bird watchers, wild flower lovers or explorers of the desert. We went on many trips together.

Many of our Arab friends, as we came to realize more and more, were engaged in welfare activities. Here there was a contrast with Israel in that the local Jordanian welfare activities were wholly financed by the people themselves, by Arabs working for Arabs, not by gifts from abroad. This is not to suggest that their welfare institutions were perfect. As in so many aspects of Arab life, there was a lack of coordination between the different organizations, but at least the effort was being made. There had been in particular a marked expansion in hospital facilities in the past few years, exemplified by the opening of the well equipped army hospital just outside the city and by the construction of a new government hospital in Jerusalem which was nearly completed when the war broke out.

While on the subject of social welfare, I might draw attention to the institution of the *waqfs* (Muslim pious funds) prevalent throughout Islam. These are trusts set up by private individuals and run by Muslim religious establishments. Some of these provide free housing for members of the donor's family, and their descendants, who may become destitute. They provide minimum amenities but are important as they do take care of the basic needs of the poorest members of the community. An example was the so-called Maghribi (Moroccan) Waqf property near the Wailing Wall, razed by the Israelis just after the war.

Among our good friends in the Old City were the Mayor, Rawhi al-Khatib, and his wife. The Mayor, whose family had lived in Jerusalem for eight hundred years, is a slight, wiry, intense man whose eyes glowed as he spoke of what he was doing to improve the condition of the city. He was utterly devoted to this goal and had spent the past ten years pursuing it. I often listened to his stories of how the Old City municipality had had to start from scratch after the 1948 war, with no water supply, no power, virtually no services of any kind. By dint of hard work he had built up the municipal administration to a point where it had become something in which he and his people could take real pride. He was not satisfied, however, but was constantly seeking new ways to develop the city under the master plan for Jerusalem and its suburbs. He is a strong Palestinian nationalist and an ardent exponent of the Arab cause, but to him the needs of the city and its inhabitants always came first.

After the war I tried to bring the two Mayors, al-Khatib and Kollek, together, as each had so many fine qualities and each was a dedicated public servant, but this proved impossible. Al-Khatib is now living in exile in Amman.

The Mayor's wife was constantly involved with civic activities and with welfare work through the Arab Women's Union. Among other things, this organization ran mother and child health clinics, a family planning clinic, and nursery schools; after the June War it ran a soup kitchen for the starving children of the city.

Among the prominent residents of the Old City were the Halabi sisters, Asia and Sophie. Asia Halabi was a remarkable woman. She had been one of the few Arab Palestinian women to enlist in the British forces during the Second World War and had risen to the rank of Major (she ran a motor pool and had acquired a thorough knowledge of vehicle maintenance). She is an amateur archaeologist of some competence and every winter was a member of the University of Pennsylvania Museum dig at Tall al-Saidiyyah in the Jordan Valley. More importantly, however, she ran a workshop for refugee women where needlework was taught, using traditional Palestinian patterns. She employed between 300 and 400 women and sent her embroideries all over the world. Her shop was one of the most important industrial establishments in Jerusalem and the quality of the work was exquisite. She and her sister Sophie, a painter with a sweet, gentle manner, lived in a house across from the Palestine Museum which commanded an excellent view of Mount Scopus. This was obviously why the house was occupied by Israeli soldiers and turned into a military strongpoint during the June War.

Dr. and Mrs. Musa Nasir were people whom we knew and admired. Dr. Nasir, a distinguished ex-Foreign Minister of the Jordanian government, is one of the older generation of Arab gentlemen who still wear the *tarbush*. He has a courtly manner and a lively sense of humor. He ran a college at Bir Zayt, a few miles outside Jerusalem, which is the only institution of higher education on the West Bank. His wife, a lady of great charm and distinction, helped her husband in running the college. She handled the administration and internal organization of the school and personally did all the housekeeping and purchasing— no mean achievement for a so-called sheltered Arab lady.

Another former Foreign Minister was Antun Atallah, a member of the Jordanian Senate and head of a bank in Jerusalem. Atallah, an impressive man with a leonine head, was inclined to read the riot act to Americans about their involvement in the Palestine question but we always remained on good terms. Like the Mayor, he is now a resident of Amman, having been exiled by the occupation authorities. We well remember that when we went to see the Atallahs immediately after the war, taking them some food and a word of comfort, their greatest distress, after all they had been through, was their inability to do anything for the one hundred or so employees of Atallah's bank, which had been closed, like all the Old City banks. It was typical of someone in Atallah's position that he should feel for these people a sense of responsibility that could only be called paternalistic. It was a part of what is known as the Arab extended family system, which helps make up for the absence in the Jordanian social fabric of many of the trappings of the modern welfare state. The same attitude was reflected in the way the Jordanians felt about their King; he was head of the family.

Finally I want to mention Anwar Nusaybah, a distinguished lawyer who had served as Governor of Jerusalem and Jordanian Ambassador to London and who returned to the Old City from London shortly before the June War. Nusaybah had lost a leg in the 1948 war but the experience did not seem to have embittered him. He was used by the Israelis as a point of contact with the Old City leaders immediately after the war.

If in giving these sketches of some of our Jordanian friends I have left the impression that they formed part of a social élite, I can only say that indeed this was a characteristic of the Old City society that we knew, and another contrast with the New City. In trying to make some generalizations about the people of the Old City and the West Bank, I would say that first of all they were intensely Palestinian and anti-Zionist. They were narrow in their outlook toward Israel and completely unaware of its achievements in developing the land, in industry, in social welfare. They were traditionalist and deeply proud of their past, but not, as some outsiders thought, wholly immersed in the past. They had their progressive side as well. They were unhappy with the government in Amman—this was especially true of the Christians. Like other Arabs they could be emotional and irrational upon occasion, but at the same time they had charm.

By way of drawing a contrast between the two civilizations in which we moved, I would emphasize that the two peoples differed sharply in background, in mental attitudes and in the way they went about their daily lives. The Israelis were modern and dynamic. They were Western in outlook and socialist by inclination. The Jordanians had the indigenous Oriental approach to life. Theirs was a traditional society in which the older values, notably those of Islam, tended to dominate. Life was more gracious and things moved at a more leisurely pace.

The differences between the Arab and Israeli cultures were to be illustrated graphically by the events of the June War. The rapid collapse of the Arab armies was facilitated by the weakness of the social links drawing the Arabs together. Arab society is dominated by individualism, by mistrust of the next man, by an inability to cooperate. Israeli society, on the other hand, is characterized by a sense of cohesiveness, a consciousness of a common destiny which during the war was enhanced by the knowledge that the Arabs' stated objective was the liquidation of Israel. One gained some glimpse into the two peoples' differing attitudes every time one drove out of the New City, or out of the Old City, into the countryside. The street corners on the Israeli side were always full of people asking for lifts all over the country—an established Israeli custom. Nothing of the sort was to be seen on the Jordanian side.

Going back and forth constantly as we did, we were very much aware of the fact that the standards of living of the two populations were far apart. After the war we assimilated the wage scale used for our local employees in the Old City to the Israeli wage scale used in the New City, and found that salaries in many instances had to be doubled. And yet our Arab driver, earning about one-half, before the war, of what our Israeli driver earned, was the owner of a small farm, with a four-room house he had built himself, and fig and olive orchards, while our Israeli driver, a recent immigrant, was housed with his large family in a rented two-room apartment in what we would call a tenement. This gives an indication of the austerity characteristic of the Israeli economy.

Another example of the same thing is that Mayor Kollek in the New City had a small walk-up apartment on the fourth floor of a building, comprising a living room with dining alcove, a small study which also served as bedroom for his daughter, and a kitchen, bedroom and bath. This modest home was occupied by one of the most prominent men in Israeli life, whose name was a household word. I do not mean to imply that Mayor al-Khatib in the Old City was housed luxuriously but he certainly had more space in which to live.

The real tragedy in the situation on both sides, however, was not that the two cultures were so different or the two standards of living were so far apart. The most striking thing about our two sets of friends was that each one had such incredible misconceptions about the other.

The Israelis tended to think of the Arabs as they had known them under the British Mandate: as for the most part a distinctly underdeveloped element in the community. They were incredulous when we told them that, during the same nineteen years that they had been consolidating their national independence, a social revolution had been taking place in the Arab world and that there were schools, hospitals and welfare institutions organized and run by the Arabs themselves in each country.

Israeli friends would sometimes ask us "Is there electricity in the Old City, or running water?" It is true that prior to 1948 the electric power and the water supply for the whole of Jerusalem had come from the New City side, but the Israelis had no conception of the Herculean efforts by which the Jordanians had succeeded in developing alternative sources. They also had no idea of the progress and relative prosperity of the Old City and the growth of a modern middle class of professional men—bankers, lawyers, teachers and the like—revolving around the basic industry: tourism. The petty merchants and shopkeepers who were so prominent a feature of the Israelis' image of the urban Arab were present but they played a less important rôle. It is worth recalling here that the economy of all Jordan was doing so well in the period before the June War that the United States decided it could progressively reduce its aid to that country. This entire picture was changed radically by the war.

The Israelis were convinced that all Arabs had only one thing in mind—the destruction of Israel—and from the propaganda put out by the Arab side this is easily understood. The collection of cartoons and quotations from the Arab press and radio published by the Israeli government in booklet form after the war gives ample confirmation of this, as did the textbooks found in the schools in Gaza, the West Bank and elsewhere. The booklet just mentioned was published by the Information Office of the Israeli Defense Force, Tel Aviv, in July 1967, and it makes disturbing reading. Page after page shows cartoons, mostly taken from the Arab press during the first part of 1967, with brave Arab soldiers annihilating panic-stricken Jews or driving them into the sea. Inflammatory statements by Jamal Abd al-Nasir and other Arab leaders are quoted extensively. As for the Arab textbooks, much of this material has been publicized by the Israelis. There is, for example, the teaching of arithmetic by asking "If there are eleven Jews and I kill six, how many Jews are left?" and so forth. No wonder the Israelis were restive.

Turning to the Arab misconceptions respecting Israel, it was plain that the Arabs knew very little of what was going on in Israel or what the Israelis were like. The Arab mood since 1948 had been one of humiliation and frustration. The Arabs regarded the immigrant Jews as interlopers who had no rights in Palestine and who had driven the refugees from their lands and their homes. They considered the Israelis to be harboring aggressive intentions toward them and to be bent on taking more Arab territory—a fear which many of them felt was borne out by the events of June 1967, and after. There was no appreciation on the part of the Arabs for what the Israelis had accomplished in the development of their country or of what the two people could do for the benefit of the entire area if it were possible for them to work together.

The Arabs' steadfast policy of boycotting Israel and of refusing to recognize its existence, on top of their own propaganda, made the gulf complete. And an inseparable part of the Arab attitude was a feeling of disillusionment and bitterness toward the West, especially the United States, for what they regarded as immoderate support of Israel and for what they termed the betrayal of their rights.

The tragedy in the situation was heightened by the fact that since 1948 a whole new generation had grown up on each side of the line knowing nothing of the other. An anecdote told me by an American Jewish friend, a resident of the New City, illustrates this. He had decided to study Arabic and had found an Israeli Arab to give him lessons. At supper one evening, he mentioned this to his family and said that the teacher would be coming to the house the next day. My friend's son, aged four and not yet in school, asked who the teacher was, and on being told, an Arab, cried out in panic, "Don't let him in the house, Daddy, he'll kill us all!"

An indication of the way in which Arab residents of the area were kept in the dark regarding Israel appeared in the Israeli press shortly after the war. An Arab refugee in the Gaza Strip, on being interviewed and asked where he came from, replied Migdal. He was told that Migdal had been incorporated into the new garden city of Ashqelon that had been built since 1948 on the Israeli sea-coast a few miles north of Gaza. He had never heard of this new city although it could not have been more than eight or ten miles away from where he had spent the past nineteen years.

After the end of hostilities, Moshe Dayan, the Israeli Minister of Defense, made a radio broadcast to which we listened, about the occupation of the West Bank, in the course of which he remarked that he had had no idea of the close economic link between the West Bank, especially the Ramallah area, and the Persian Gulf, or of the fact that remittances sent back to the West Bank by breadwinners in the Gulf were an important element in Jordan's balance of payments. That so basic a feature of the Jordanian West Bank economy should not have been known across the line a few miles away is suggestive.

Again, after the war, the doctors at Hadassah Hospital invited a group of Old City doctors to come over and see the new hospital and stay for lunch. Present were several Hadassah ladies, one of whom kept opening her purse, passing around ballpoint pens and chewing gum, and asking the visiting Jordanians if they had ever seen anything of this sort. And these were Westernized professional men, for the most part graduates of the American University of Beirut, many holding advanced degrees from Europe or America.

It might be pertinent to record that those Israelis whom we knew showed more disposition to ask us about the other side, and to discuss the basic issues in an effort to find a solution, than did our Jordanian contacts. In three years I can recall only a very few talks with Arab friends, out of many that I had on the subject of the Arab-Israel dispute, which reflected a realistic and dispassionate attitude on their part or recognized the need for some sort of accommodation.

In spite of the prevailing atmosphere, however, it would not be correct to say that the people we knew personally on either side were aggressive or violent toward those on the other side. In Israel we frequently heard the hope expressed that hostilities could be avoided. And even among the refugees in Jordan, where support for Ahmad Shuqayri and his Palestine Liberation Organization could be expected to be strong, there was very little talk of actually picking up a rifle and rushing to free the "usurped homeland." The bloodthirsty and violent propaganda was mainly confined to the radio and press and was rarely if ever voiced to us privately. However, it was significant that not one of our Jordanian friends had sons in the armed forces whereas all our Israeli friends did—and daughters, too. The explanation lies not only in the fact that Israel has a citizen army and Jordan a professional army, but also in the different concepts of patriotism or national loyalty held on either side of the line.

This account of Jerusalem's people cannot stop with a description of only the Jewish and Arab residents of the city. For Jerusalem is not simply an Arab city or a Jewish city or a city with Arab and Jewish inhabitants; it is an international city and a world religious and historical center. And the international community which has been attracted to Jerusalem over the years by the peculiar character of the city is a part of the Jerusalem scene and indeed has served in some ways to shape the city into the Jerusalem we know. I therefore must give some treatment to these foreign residents: first the Consular Corps of which I was a member, then the ecclesiastical leaders, the representatives of the United Nations, and the other members of the international community.

The Jerusalem Consular Corps is an institution with a history going back to Ottoman times (our own representation dates from 1857). The Corps embodied the Christian interest in the Holy Places and it maintained close contact with the ecclesiastical leaders in the city. As in other parts of the Middle East, consuls used to be figures of some importance. They were preceded along the street by a *kavass*, or consular guard, wearing an elaborate braided uniform with baggy Turkish trousers and carrying a gold-tipped staff which he used to clear a path for the dignitary.

In more recent times, much of this pageantry has faded into history, although the Corps in Jerusalem still regards itself as having a standing of some importance in the community. Occasionally the Corps would make representations to the local authorities regarding some interference with access to the Holy Places. During the crisis in May 1967, leading to the June War, the consuls met and decided to recommend to their governments that in the event of hostilities Jerusalem should be declared an open city (unfortunately events moved too fast for this to have any effect). In general, however, it can be said that the main activities of the Corps were ceremonial, such as putting in an appearance at the public celebration of religious festivals.

The composition of the Consular Corps had altered after the 1948 Palestine war and the partition of the city, since not all members had the unlimited crossing privilege. In fact there were three categories into which the members of the Corps fell: those like our British, French and other Western colleagues (and ourselves) whose countries supported the concept of an internationalized Jerusalem and who had the crossing privilege; those who resided in the Old City and could not cross to the Israeli side (our Arab colleagues); and those who lived in the New City and could not cross to the Jordanian side without filing an application once or twice a month, in the same manner as members of the Embassies in Tel Aviv.

During the June War, those of our Arab colleagues who had not left had a difficult time when Israeli troops overran the Old City. They had taken asylum with our Belgian colleague and were forcibly removed and taken to a place of detention. This was because Israel had no diplomatic relations with any of the Arab countries and in fact was legally in a state of war with them from 1948 on. This incident led to a stiff protest by Belgium to Israel. Some of the Arab representatives were subsequently released but several were still in custody when we left Jerusalem.

Of the nine consular representatives of the first category, those who had the crossing privilege and maintained two offices, only two, the British and the Spanish, had their principal residence in the Old City. The remainder (like myself) were based in the New City. The Arabs were very critical of the fact that so many of us happened to reside in the Israeli sector, and indeed on one occasion the Jordanian Prime Minister summoned our Ambassador to complain of this. Fortunately the Ambassador was able to put matters in proper perspective but this remained as a potential source of friction.

As one of the main duties of the Consular Corps was to maintain contact with the ecclesiastical leaders in Jerusalem, it would next seem appropriate to say something about ecclesiastical Jerusalem. When I first went there before World War II, I found that our office maintained an official (the late Edward W. Blatchford) who was popularly called the "ecclesiastical attaché" and whose job it was to follow developments in the religious sphere. This position no longer existed by the time I returned as Consul General in 1964, but the ecclesiastical contacts which our office was called upon to maintain were still extensive.

In addition to the Muslim and Jewish dignitaries, Jerusalem was the seat of a sizeable number of Christian prelates, including three patriarchs, two archbishops, three bishops, two patriarchal vicars, and several lesser figures, each one representing—and this is the point—a different sect. There was also the Franciscan *Custos*, whose position embodied the fact that for centuries the Franciscans had had the custody of those Christian shrines where the so-called "Latins" (the Roman Catholics) had rights. The Custos, incidentally, was addressed as "Your Paternity," whereas the three Patriarchs (Latin, Greek and Armenian) were addressed as "Your Beatitude."

The lesser sects included the Copts, the Syrian Orthodox or Jacobites, and the so-called Uniate churches (those which had reverted to communion with Rome), such as the Greek, Syrian, Coptic, Armenian and Chaldean Catholics. There were also the Ethiopian or Abyssinian Copts who were allowed by the other sects to worship only on the roof of the Church of the Holy Sepulchre, and the Protestants. The latter included the Anglicans, who had originally shared a bishop in rotation with the Prussian Lutherans (a curious arrangement, which the Prince Consort, Queen Victoria's husband, had promoted). Now the Anglicans have an archbishop of their own, after a lapse of some years in the nineteenth century which led to the vacant see's being known as the "dead see." The Protestants also included the Scots Presbyterians, who had a handsome church located in the New City near Mount Zion.

The ecclesiastical scene in Jerusalem was complicated by the situation pertaining to the Russian churches. For centuries prior to the 1917 revolution the Russian Orthodox Church had been active in the Holy Land and had owned extensive properties. Since the revolution there had been a dispute between the adherents of the Russian Church controlled by the Metropolitan of Moscow (subordinate to the Soviet régime, of course) and those of the so-called expatriate Russian Church which is White Russian and has headquarters in New York City.

The Israeli government had recognized the claim of the Soviet Russian Church to the Russian Orthodox properties in Israel, including the large Russian compound in the New City, and had agreed to purchase most of these properties from the Soviet government. In Jordan, the situation was entirely different. The government, although it had recognized the Soviet Union, continued to recognize the expatriate church in New York as the owner of the Russian Orthodox properties in the Old City. Our Consulate was involved in this aspect of the matter since the representatives of the expatriate church were American citizens. At one point, in fact, I was asked by them if I would take over their properties in the Old City to prevent a seizure by the Moscow Church which they feared was going to occur. Fortunately it did not, as I had no such authority.

One result of this situation was that in the New City there was an Archimandrite, the Archimandrite Germogen, who was under the Metropolitan of Moscow and to all intents and purposes a member of the Soviet diplomatic mission in Israel. As often as he could, that is once or twice a month, he would apply for permission to pass through the Mandelbaum Gate to the Old City, ostensibly to maintain contact with the Russian Orthodox clergy in the Old City but actually, it was suspected, to engage in subversive activities. Ironically, he had to apply for this permission through the Greek Orthodox Patriarch, who was strongly anti-Communist. It was this same Patriarch who had objected violently to the assignment, shortly after Jordan recognized the Soviet Union, of a representative of the Moscow Church to the Old City. This individual was eventually expelled from Jordan.

The venerable prelates (many of them were of advanced years) who represented the various sects added a colorful element to the local scene, although we sometimes gained the impression that their energies were principally directed toward jealously guarding their rights in the different Holy Places against the encroachments, real or imagined, of the other Christian groups. While the energies of the Christian leaders were thus often diverted into quarrels, the prelates were at their best when officiating at the many Christian ceremonies which were so prominent a feature of life in the Holy City. The most colorful of these is the Ceremony of the Holy Fire, celebrated at the Church of the Holy Sepulchre on the Greek Orthodox and Armenian Easter Eve. It was first described by the Breton monk, Bernard the Wise, in the year 870, and by many subsequent travellers, notably by Robert Curzon in his book *Monasteries of the Levant* written over a hundred years ago. In this ceremony, the faithful throng to seize the "Holy Fire" (supposedly coming from Heaven) from a torch lit by the Patriarch, and then spread the flame from person to person throughout the church. This has often led to rioting and even bloodshed. There is also the curious rite, performed with great pomp by the Ethiopians on Easter Eve on the roof of the Church, of "searching for the body of the Lord."

A Christian occurrence of a rather special nature which took place during my stay in Jerusalem was the reinterring of the remains of Mar Saba (Saint Saba), who had died in the year 532 and whose remains had been in Italy for many centuries. The Consular Corps was invited by the Greek Orthodox Patriarch to a mass at the Holy Sepulchre, featuring the somewhat grisly presence, in a glass coffin, of the saint himself in a mummified state. He was later removed to the Convent of Mar Saba in the desert between Jerusalem and the Dead Sea, which he had founded in the sixth century.

The United Nations was represented in Jerusalem by UNTSO (the United Nations Truce Supervision Organization) and UNRWA (the United Nations Relief and Works Agency for Palestine Refugees in the Near East). The former, which had its headquarters at Government House, in the no-man's land just south of Jerusalem, had a staff of some 135 military observers, drawn from twelve countries, and an equal number of civilian advisers and administrative personnel (an example of Parkinson's Law). The military observers were deployed along the Armistice lines at various points and were rotated in and out of headquarters (see Chapter V).

We became very familiar with the sight of the UNTSO officers with their blue berets and their white vehicles with a large "UN" painted on the sides. The members of UNTSO had the crossing privilege, so that we frequently met at Mandelbaum Gate. Most of them seemed to prefer to live in the Jordanian sector although a few lived in the New City. Only the Chief of Staff, Lt. Gen. Odd Bull, a distinguished-looking Norwegian Air Force officer with a handsome Swedish wife, resided at Government House.

We saw a good deal of General Bull and the senior members of his staff, notably his American deputy, who during most of our stay in the city was Colonel Floyd M. Johnson, Jr., of the US Marines, a Texan who at six feet six towered above us all. His wife Alice was a former journalist who had had the distinction of being the first woman to be employed by the *Wall Street Journal*. Among General Bull's principal advisers was the fabulous Henri Vigier, a Frenchman who had been with UNTSO from its inception in 1948 and before that with the League of Nations, starting in about 1922. Vigier, an octogenarian with a keen mind and an incredibly detailed knowledge of Armistice affairs, was known as the "Old Fox" and was seldom bested in an argument by either Arabs or Israelis.

The members of UNRWA were less prominent on the Jerusalem scene. Their headquarters were in Beirut, not Jerusalem, and their international as distinct from their local staff numbered only three or four. These did not have the crossing privilege and were confined to the Old City. And while UNEF (the United Nations Emergency Force, see Chapter IV) operated out of Gaza rather than Jerusalem, a frequent visitor to the city was UNEF's commander, the Indian

General Indar Jit Rikhye, a most colorful and impressive officer in the mold of the British Indian Army, who liked to come and stay with General Bull at Government House.

A segment of the international community of whom we saw a good deal were the archaeologists. In the New City we had the Hebrew Union College Biblical and Archaeological School, with headquarters in the States, under the overall direction of an old friend, Nelson Glueck. We had known him since 1940 when he had headed the American School of Oriental Research in the Old City. Dr. Glueck was a frequent visitor to Jerusalem and was there just after the June War, when it was a source of great satisfaction for him to be able once again to visit the Old City and the American School. Hebrew Union College ran an archaeological dig at Gezer in the coastal plain, which we often visited with Dr. Glueck, Ernest Wright, or William Dever, the resident head of the school, who became virtually an honorary member of our staff and our household during the trying days of the war when his wife Norma was working for me as a temporary secretary.

Our archaeologist friends in the Old City were at the American and British Schools and at the French *Ecole Biblique,* the latter a world-renowned center of Biblical studies where we attended many lectures given by Père Roland de Vaux, the great authority on the Dead Sea Scrolls, and the other fathers. We also made frequent trips into the surrounding country with these archaeologists. Indeed, our association with them was a leading feature of our life in Jerusalem and a constant intellectual stimulus. I would include in this group Canon John Zimmerman of the Anglican Cathedral, a former chaplain in the US Navy and a Biblical scholar of considerable authority. We used to say he was the best guide we knew to the Old City.

The most prominent of our own citizens in the Old City was Mrs. Bertha Spafford Vester (recently deceased at the age of 90) who had been a resident of Jerusalem since 1881 and had many tales to tell of her experiences over the years, starting with the time General "Chinese" Gordon dandled her on his knee on one of his visits to the Holy City and going on through General Allenby's arrival in the starving, beleaguered city in 1917 to more modern days. She lived through two more wars in Jerusalem (1948 and 1967) and was a woman of indomitable character. The Vester family ran the American Colony, (a hotel, shop, and travel agency) and the Spafford Memorial Hospital (for children)—both of them established Jerusalem institutions, with Jordanian as well as American participation. Mrs. Vester was an exact contemporary of Mrs. Beatrice Magnes and we used to pass greetings back and forth between these two great ladies. After the war, they met again and had many reminiscences to exchange.

So much, then, for the Jerusalem we knew. It would next seem useful to take a look at the historical background, and try to gain some understanding of the bitter dispute that has plagued the Holy Land for so many years.

IV

The Background

Anyone who attempts to summarize the history of the Palestine problem must approach the task with some trepidation. As the late George Antonius pointed out in his classic account of the Arab national movement, *The Arab Awakening:*[1]

> For the historian, the study of the Palestine problem is beset with particular difficulties. In the first place, the material is enormous and widely scattered. In the second place, it is to an unusual degree conflicting and inconsistent. Thirdly, a large proportion of it which on inspection appears relevant and promising turns out, when sifted, to rest upon false assumptions and questionable data. Lastly, the passions aroused by Palestine have done so much to obscure the truth that the facts have become enveloped in a mist of sentiment, legend and propaganda, which acts as a smoke-screen of almost impenetrable density.

And yet it is particularly important to have some grasp of the historical background of the Palestine case if we are to understand how the present impasse came about. In the words of the Peel Commission (1937), "no other problem of our time is so deeply rooted in the past."[2]

Until the First World War, there was no Palestine problem. Basically, the problem stems from the fact that when the British conquered Palestine from the Turks, the Arabs were in the overwhelming majority in the country. It was the introduction, under the terms of the Balfour Declaration and the Mandate, of Jewish immigrants in such numbers as to lead the Arabs of Palestine to believe they were threatened—as well as betrayed—that caused the conflict, a conflict that is not yet resolved. And an inseparable part of the problem lies in the contradictory nature of the promises regarding the future of Palestine which the British had made during their wartime negotiations with the Arabs, with the Jews, and with the French and their other Allies, at the same time as President Wilson's Fourteen Points gave expression to a

---

[1] Antonius, *The Arab Awakening*, p. 386.
[2] *Palestine, Royal Commission Report*, 1937, Cmd. 5479, p. 2.

rising spirit of national self determination. The problem is still with us today, after three wars (1948, 1956 and 1967) and after all the grief and passion and strife that have afflicted this unhappy land.

When the First World War broke out, the population of Palestine, according to the best available estimates, was around 689,000, of whom some 85,000 were Jews and the remainder were Arabs. Thus the Arabs constituted some 88 per cent of the inhabitants.[3] With the awakening of Arab nationalism that took place in the late nineteenth and early twentieth centuries, the Arabs of Palestine were beginning to regard the land as their country and they have done so ever since.

In 1915, the British, anxious to gain Arab support in the war against Turkey, exchanged letters (known as the McMahon Correspondence) with the Sharif Husayn of Mecca regarding the terms and conditions under which the Arab people, for whom he acted as spokesman, would enter the war. The Arabs asked that in return for their entry into the war the British should recognize their independence. While the wording of the basic British commitment (dated October 24, 1915) is unfortunately vague as to the precise area that would become independent after the war (see appendix A) the Arabs understood, and have continued to claim, that Palestine was included in this area. And they were not disabused of this belief by additional assurances which they received later in the war.

In keeping with their agreement with the British, the Arabs launched their revolt in June 1916 and contributed significantly to the war effort against the Turks. By early 1918, more Turkish troops were engaged against Arab forces than against British forces. At the end of the war, the entire area within the precise boundaries outlined by the Sharif of Mecca as encompassing the region in which Arab independence would be recognized had been liberated and the Arabs felt they had fulfilled their part of the bargain.

The British, however, also made a wartime commitment to the Jews, whose connection with Palestine had never been broken from antiquity

---

[3] There was no census in Palestine before the British census of 1922, so it is necessary to rely on estimates for earlier years. The *Survey of Palestine,* prepared by the government of Palestine for the Anglo-American Committee of Inquiry in 1946, states that according to Turkish estimates the population in 1914 totaled 689,000, of whom 84,660 were Jews (this would be about 12%). The *Survey* also states that the 1922 census showed the "settled" population to be 649,048, of whom 486,177 were Muslims, 83,790 Jews and 71,464 Christians (there was also a total population figure including nomads of 752,048 but this is not generally used). According to the *Survey,* it is estimated that the Jewish population of the country fell to 56,000 during the First World War, as a result of epidemics, emigration and deportation by the Turks. This would suggest that at the time of the Balfour Declaration in 1917, the proportion of Jews was only about nine per cent.

and whose interest in the land had been enhanced by the rise of Zionism. During the early part of the war, the Zionists in Great Britain, notably Chaim Weizmann, who was doing war work for the British Admiralty, were in frequent touch with leaders of the government with a view to persuading them of the desirability of some expression of official sympathy with Jewish aspirations respecting Palestine. In this effort the Zionists were helped by the fact that many British statesmen were deeply imbued with Biblical lore and with a belief that the Christians of the world had an obligation toward the Jews, that to assist the Jews to return to the Holy Land would be an act of reparation. Indeed, it was Prime Minister David Lloyd George who said he was brought up to name all the kings of Israel but not those of England. The Zionists were also aided by the force of Weizmann's personality. Years later he made a powerful impression on the Anglo-American Committee of Inquiry, before which he testified in 1946.

On November 2, 1917, the Foreign Secretary, Arthur Balfour, wrote a letter to the head of the British Zionist Federation stating what has come to be known as the Balfour Declaration. This said, in language that seems deliberately vague (see appendix B) that His Majesty's government favored the "establishment in Palestine of a national home for the Jewish people," on condition that nothing be done to "prejudice the civil and religious rights of existing non-Jewish communities in Palestine or the rights and political status enjoyed by Jews in any other country." Here again the principal motivation of the government seems to have been to win the war, by enlisting the support of the influential Jewish communities in England, the United States and elsewhere.

It was not only to the Arabs and Jews, however, that the British made wartime pledges involving Palestine. In the course of secret negotiations during 1915-1916 between Great Britain, France and Imperial Russia, regarding the disposition of the territories of the Ottoman Empire after the war, it was agreed that Palestine should be placed under international administration. This agreement, to which Italy adhered in 1917 and which was designed to carve out spheres of influence in the Middle East, is called the Sykes-Picot Agreement (see appendix C). To the great embarrassment of the Allies, it was made public by the Bolsheviks after the October Revolution, along with other secret archives. The British in this instance again seem to have been motivated largely by strategic considerations: by a belief that an international régime would offer a means of protecting Palestine,

which the British regarded as strategically important, against the encroachments of the French in Syria next door.

While today we might find it hard to believe that the British were
able to enter almost simultaneously into these conflicting commitments
(which led some observers to refer to the Promised Land as the "Too-
Promised Land") it would be too much to say that they were guilty of
deliberate fraud. It is true that they failed to let everyone involved
know the full extent of the pledges they had made. But the simple
explanation seems to have been that there was an extraordinary lack of
coordination within the British government. There was, for instance,
no single Cabinet Minister who knew all the details of all three sets of
negotiations. The whole emphasis in London was on winning the war,
and the government's actions were characterized by haste, confusion
and imprecision.

There was also an almost complete lack of knowledge as to the
actual situation in Palestine. Practically no one seems to have realized
that the "existing non-Jewish communities" mentioned by Balfour
represented nearly 90 per cent of the inhabitants at the beginning of
the war. And in any event the prevailing impression among those few
who were knowledgeable about the country was that there was every
reason to anticipate that the Arabs would welcome the coming of the
Jews, bringing with them the blessings of Western civilization. Indeed
this was the attitude of some Arabs at first, though it quickly changed.

Of the three undertakings in which the British became involved
with respect to Palestine, the Sykes-Picot Agreement was considered
to have lapsed as a result of Russia's withdrawal from the war. Moreover, in the postwar settlement, France concurred in the assumption by
the British of responsibility for Palestine, in return for concessions
elsewhere. The pledges to the Arabs and the Jews, however, remained
to plague British administrators during the more than thirty years that
they governed the country. In fact, it can be said that they had undertaken an impossible task. How, indeed, to establish a national home
(whatever that meant) in Palestine for the Jewish people (however
defined) without affecting the rights of the great majority of the
population, was a problem which the British were never able to solve.

To continue with the story, British forces under Allenby entered
Jerusalem in December 1917, and by the next summer all Palestine
had been freed of Turkish rule and placed under British military
administration. At the outset, Arab leaders did not display too much
concern as to the implications of the Balfour Declaration. In fact, the
Amir Faysal, a son of the Sharif of Mecca who had been prominent in

the Arab Revolt and in the movement for independence, held two meetings with Dr. Weizmann, and signed an agreement with him providing for the implementation of the Balfour Declaration and for the encouragement of immigration of Jews into Palestine on a large scale. Faysal, however, made his concurrence conditional upon the fulfillment by the British of their pledges regarding independence, and the agreement with Weizmann of course fell through.

During the Paris Peace Conference in 1919 there was considerable discussion of the ex-Turkish territories and of their disposition. President Wilson, becoming concerned at a possible conflict between Allied wartime commitments and his Fourteen Points, proposed that an Allied Commission be sent to the Middle East to sound out the desires of the inhabitants of the region. From this proposal materialized not an Allied but a solely American commission, known as the King-Crane Commission from the names of its two members, Henry C. King and Charles R. Crane. This commission spent several months in the area and submitted a report to President Wilson but the report did not reach Washington until after he had left on his trip West in behalf of the League of Nations, during which came his collapse, and there is no evidence that he ever saw it. At all events, it was pigeon-holed by the American government and ignored by the Allies.

The King-Crane Commission recommended a "serious modification of the extreme Zionist program" of unlimited immigration of Jews, which was described as having the ultimate aim of making Palestine into a Jewish state. The commissioners considered that the creation of a Jewish state could not be accomplished without the "gravest trespass" upon the rights of the Arab population, whom they had found to be "emphatically against the entire Zionist program." They also stated that if Palestine were to become a Jewish state the Christians and Muslims would not be satisfied to have their Holy Places in Jewish hands. Finally, they recommended that Palestine should form a single mandate with Syria, and they reported that the vast majority of the people of the area would prefer to have the United States as the Mandatory.

Following the Peace Conference, a meeting of the Allies at San Remo in 1920 allocated the various mandates under the system established in the Covenant of the League of Nations, and agreed that the Mandate for Palestine should be held by Great Britain. It was stipulated that the Mandatory should be responsible for putting into effect the Balfour Declaration. The text of the Mandate was approved by the Council of the League of Nations in 1923; the British of course had been in control of Palestine since 1917 and had replaced the military administration with a civil government in 1920, when the first British High Commissioner, Sir Herbert Samuel, a Jew and a distinguished public servant, had arrived. It had not been at all certain that Great Britain would receive the Mandate for Palestine, as many Roman Catholic powers were not enthusiastic about having a Protestant power in charge of the Holy Places, but the Zionists carried on a persistent and successful campaign in favor of the British.

The Mandate for Palestine[4] is a unique document. Its preamble repeated the entire text of the Balfour Declaration, adding, in language somewhat stronger than the Declaration itself, that "recognition has thereby been given to the historical connection of the Jewish people with Palestine and the grounds for reconstituting their national home in that country." It has been argued that the Balfour Declaration was inconsistent with Article 22 of the Covenant of the League, which states that certain communities formerly part of the Ottoman Empire had "reached a stage of development where their existence as independent nations can be provisionally recognized . . . the wishes of these communities must be a principal consideration in the selection of the Mandatory." Unlike the other mandates covering the former Turkish territories, the Mandate for Palestine made no provision for its termination. The Mandatory was made responsible for "placing the country under such political, administrative and economic conditions as will secure the establishment of the Jewish national home" and was enjoined to "facilitate Jewish immigration" and encourage "close settlement by Jews on the land," while protecting the rights of other sections of the population, who were nowhere identified. An "appropriate Jewish agency" was to be set up for the purpose of advising and cooperating with the administration in such matters as might affect the establishment of the Jewish national home and the interests of the Jewish population. It was provided that the Zionist organization should be recognized as such agency provided it met certain requirements. Hebrew, as well as Arabic and English, would be an official language (although at the time it hardly existed), and each community could maintain its own schools.

There was a reference to the "development of self-governing institutions" but this was not further spelled out as in the other mandates.

---

[4] The text of the Mandate may be found in Hurewitz, *Diplomacy in the Near and Middle East*, in the Report of the Anglo-American Committee of Inquiry and in many other places. The text of the Covenant of the League of Nations may also be found in many sources, e.g., Felix Morley, *The Society of Nations*.

There were also provisions regarding free access to the Holy Places and the appointment of a special commission for the sites.

From this summary of the main clauses of the Palestine Mandate it can be seen that it was drawn up with the primary purpose of facilitating Zionist objectives. At the same time it attempted to protect the rights of the Arabs: a conflict of interests which led the Peel Commission to report in 1937 that the Mandate was unworkable.

The British announced (in 1922) that the clauses of the Mandate regarding the Jewish national home would not be applied in Trans-Jordan (which was included in the Mandate). This served somewhat to console the Arabs but they remained bitter at many aspects of the postwar settlement, especially their failure to gain the independence that they felt had been promised them throughout the former Turkish territories. The Jews also suffered some disappointments, not only with regard to Trans-Jordan but also with regard to the Litani Valley in Lebanon, which with its water resources they had hoped to have included in the area of the Palestine Mandate.[5]

The early years of the Mandate were relatively uneventful, largely because there was no substantial Jewish immigration. In fact during the late 1920s immigration nearly dried up and was running at not much more than 2,000 per year: in 1927 emigrants actually exceeded immigrants, and in 1928 came within 10 of doing so. As early as 1920, however, there had been Arab disturbances and these continued as the Arabs became more vocal in their opposition to the Jewish national home. By 1922 the British government had begun to realize that there was a conflict between the aspirations of the Arabs and those of the Jews and had issued a statement of policy which denied that the purpose of the government was to create a wholly Jewish Palestine.[6] It was pointed out that the Balfour Declaration did not provide that

---

[5] The Zionists had submitted, under date of February 3, 1919, a memorandum to the Paris Peace Conference asking that the boundaries of Palestine be extended northwards to the Mediterranean coast near Sidon, thence eastwards across Mount Hermon to the Hijaz Railway and thence southwards to Aqaba. This would have meant that substantial portions of southern Lebanon, southern Syria and western Trans-Jordan would have been included in the area in which the Jewish national home would apply. See Barbour, *Palestine—Star or Crescent?*, p. 119; Frischwasser-Ra'anan, *Frontiers of a Nation*, p. 107; and Polk, Stamler, and Asfour, *Backdrop to Tragedy*, p. 74.

[6] The text of the 1922 White Paper on Palestine, Cmd. 1700, (often called the Churchill White Paper as Winston Churchill was Colonial Secretary at the time) may be found in Hurewitz, *op. cit.*

Palestine should be converted into a Jewish national home but that such a home should be founded *in Palestine.*[7]

Early in the Mandate years there began to develop a gulf between the Arab and Jewish communities. The Jews had the advantage over the Arabs of being better educated and of having the support of world Jewry in building up their national home. Their wage scales were higher than those of the Arab community. They began almost at once to develop their own institutions to an extent that made the Jewish community a state within a state, with their own executive (the Jewish Agency), legislature (the National Council or *Vaad Leumi*), trade union system (the *Histadrut*), welfare services, schools, and even their own military organization (the *Haganah,* originally set up for the defense of Jewish settlements). So well organized, in fact, were the Jews that everyone who followed the Palestine scene knew, years before the Jewish state came into being, that Weizmann would be the President, Ben Gurion the Prime Minister, Shertok (Sharett) the Foreign Minister, and so on.

The Arabs for their part were divided into factions and failed entirely to develop an effective community organization. Daily their resentment grew as they observed the progress the Jews were making. They were particularly bitter at the fact that the Jews refused to employ Arab labor on Jewish-owned land or in Jewish enterprises. Thus from the very start the seeds of the division of the country into two camps were sown. Meanwhile several efforts on the part of the Mandatory administration to set up a legislative council or other self-governing institutions failed, because of opposition from one community or the other, and this tended to intensify the split. Arab attacks on Jews continued and in 1929 and 1930 there were serious clashes.

The situation with respect to immigration changed markedly in the 1930s, with the threat and then the reality of Hitler's assuming power in Germany. Indeed, it can be stated that if it had not been for the rise of Nazi Germany there would not have been a Jewish state in Palestine. In 1935, immigration was as high as 62,000. By 1939 the Jews, who in the first census of 1922 had totaled 84,000, or 13 per cent out of a population of 649,000, totaled 450,000, or 30 per cent out of a population of one and a half million.[8]

---

[7] It was only after the Zionist Organization gave an assurance that it would be bound by this statement of policy that it was recognized by the British government as the "appropriate Jewish agency" envisaged in the Mandate.

[8] Figures on Jewish immigration from 1920 through 1946 are given in *The Political History of Palestine Under British Administration,* prepared by the British government in 1947 for the United Nations Special Committee on Palestine.

The Arabs of Palestine reacted to the increased immigration of Jews by launching a campaign of outright terrorism. By 1936 the situation had deteriorated to such an extent that the British government appointed a Royal Commission (the Peel Commission) to examine the problem. It was this commission, in a masterly report that still repays reading, that declared the Mandate to be unworkable. It stated: "To put it in one sentence, we cannot—in Palestine as it now is—both concede the Arab claim to self-government and secure the establishment of the Jewish national home."

The solution put forward by the Peel Commission was the termination of the Mandate and the partition of the country into Arab and Jewish states, with a Jerusalem enclave remaining under British administration. A second commission (the Woodhead Commission) was sent out in 1938 to devise a specific plan of partition but reported that it was unable to agree on a practical one.[9]

The British then convened a "Round Table Conference" in London (actually an Anglo-Jewish and an Anglo-Arab conference as the Arabs refused to sit at the same table with the Jews) but no agreement was forthcoming. The result was that in May 1939 the British issued a White Paper[10] outlining the government's views on the future of the country in an attempt to put an end to uncertainty as to the objectives of British policy.

The White Paper declared unequivocally that it was not part of British policy that Palestine should become a Jewish state. Nor did the McMahon Correspondence justify the view that it should be converted into an Arab state. The White Paper set as the British goal the termination of the Mandate within ten years and the establishment of an independent Palestine state in which both Arabs and Jews would participate. Meanwhile, a quota was set up for Jewish immigration over the next five years, after which no further Jewish immigration would be permitted without the consent of the Arabs of Palestine. It was also provided that the administration would issue regulations prohibiting or regulating the sale of land to Jews.

The White Paper was bitterly attacked by Jewish opinion as a betrayal of the Balfour Declaration and of the Mandate and as a transparent attempt to appease the Arabs (who in the period immediately before the Second World War were being actively wooed by the Axis powers). Winston Churchill, an avowed pro-Zionist, declared that it was the "end of the dream." The Permanent Mandates Commission of

[9] *Palestine, Partition Commission Report*, 1938, Cmd. 5854.
[10] The 1939 White Paper may be found in Hurewitz.

the League of Nations examined the White Paper and concluded that it was not in accordance with the Commission's interpretation of the Mandate. And even the Arabs of Palestine were not satisfied, as they considered the period of transition before self-government to be too long and in any event had become distrustful of British intentions. As a matter of fact, it is hard to deny that the White Paper was a repudiation of the Jewish national home; though it is understandable that the British, faced with the increasingly irreconcilable positions of the parties to the dispute and conscious of the need to have the support of the Arab world in the coming confrontation with the Axis, should take the line that they did.

From then on, the development of the National Home was crystallized on the existing basis, with only a minimum amount (15,000) of Jewish immigration permitted each year and with growing hostility on the part of the Jews toward the British administration. On the outbreak of the Second World War, the country became relatively quiet as the emphasis shifted elsewhere, to the Western Desert and to Hitler's Europe, where the systematic annihilation of millions of Jews shocked the conscience of mankind and convinced many, both Jews and non-Jews, that the Jews had to have a state of their own. In fact, it was in 1942, in the midst of the war, at a Zionist convention at the Biltmore Hotel in New York City, that the movement, for the first time in Zionist history, came out officially for the creation of a Jewish state in Palestine. It was only six years until the goal of the Biltmore Program was attained: a remarkable achievement indeed.[11]

Toward the end of the war, as the British government continued to give no sign of repealing the White Paper or of having any other solution in mind for the basic problems of the country, terrorism and illegal immigration by Jews developed on a wide basis. The causes were the White Paper itself, with its implied refutation of a fundamental article of faith for Zionists that all Jews had the right to go to Palestine, and the Holocaust, the slaughter of the Jews in Europe. These two factors combined to promote among the Jewish community a feeling of disillusionment and despair, even of desperation, and the conviction grew that they had to take matters into their own hands.

As Europe began to be liberated, great pressure was brought to bear on the British government to open up Palestine to the survivors of the concentration camps. And this brings us to the first really active inter-

[11] The Biltmore Program (May 11, 1942) is given in Khouri, *The Arab-Jewish Dilemma*, p. 362. Starting about 1940, according to Ben Gurion, the major focus of Zionist pressure shifted from London to New York and Washington.

vention of the government of the United States in the Palestine problem.

It can be said that it was not until the mid-1940s that the United States was called upon to have more than a vague attitude toward Palestine. It was true that our interest in the country went back at least as far as Woodrow Wilson, although an 1818 statement by former President John Adams, expressing a wish to see the Jews "again in Judea, an independent nation" has been unearthed. It was also true that every President, beginning with Wilson, had gone on record as affirming support for the National Home and that this was the purport of a resolution passed by Congress in 1922.[12] Most Americans, if asked, would probably have said that the Jewish people should be allowed to return to their ancient homeland as the Bible said they should (as recently as the fall of 1968 a prominent American evangelist said exactly this in reply to a query). Most Americans, further, knew very little if anything about the Middle East, and not one in a million was aware that at the time of the First World War the Jews were only a small minority in Palestine.

The isolationism which characterized our foreign relations in the 1920s and 1930s contributed to our playing a minor rôle in Middle Eastern affairs. Moreover, at this time the interest of American Jews in Palestine was minimal and consequently they did not bring much pressure to bear on the American government to follow a particular line of policy. This served to keep in the background the basic dilemma which our policy faced. The dilemma, however, was already in being. It is undeniable that American Jews have been influenced over the years in their voting behavior by the views expressed by candidates for political office toward the Palestine question, and that Jews hold a pivotal position in certain cities and hence in certain states. On the other hand, such stake as we had in the Middle East at the time seemed to be more on the Arab side than the Jewish: our commercial interests, our missionaries and educators (going back to the mid-nineteenth century, the American University of Beirut, for example, having been founded in 1866)—all these combined to start us off on a good footing with the Arab world in the years following World War I. It is thus easy to understand that our policymakers, sensing no doubt the essential conflict between the Jewish and the Arab interests in Palestine, should have perferred to have us stand on the sidelines and leave this particular headache to the British.

---

[12] The texts of pro-Zionist statements by various US Presidents and of the 1922 Congressional Resolution are given in Gervasi, *The Case for Israel*, p. 197-201.

That Palestine was a British responsibility was, in fact, the attitude of Secretary of State Cordell Hull toward the problem in the 1930s and 1940s. He says so in his memoirs and he repeatedly used this phrase in answering inquiries from Senators and others. When I took over the State Department's Palestine desk in 1943 this was the formula we used in such instances. In replying to Arab leaders who expressed concern regarding Zionist aims, we also employed a statement to the effect that no decision regarding the "basic situation" in Palestine should be taken without "full consultation with both Arabs and Jews." As can readily be seen, this wording, which was also used by the British at the time, was very loose and subject to different interpretations.

Thus it was possible for a President, when (as occurred from time to time) he had been induced to give some pledge of support to a Zionist group, to assure Arab leaders that this did not denote any change in the "basic situation." It was even possible for President Franklin D. Roosevelt in his meeting with King Abd al-Aziz Ibn Saud after Yalta in early 1945 to assure the King that he would do nothing to help the Jews against the Arabs (this pledge was put in writing just before the President's death, and the letter was subsequently made public: see appendix D).

It should be emphasized that the correspondence carried out by President Roosevelt and after him by President Harry S Truman with Arab leaders in an effort to reassure them by use of the "full consultation" formula was done with the specific authorization of the President in each instance. It was not a case, as has been alleged, of the State Department's sending out messages behind the President's back.[13]

In 1944, resolutions were introduced into both Houses of Congress, at Zionist instigation, urging that there be unrestricted Jewish immigration into Palestine and that Palestine should eventually become a Jewish state. There were strong protests from the Arabs and considerable anxiety was felt in the executive branch of the government. Secretary Hull was reluctant to intervene publicly but Secretary of War Stimson and Chief of Staff Marshall told Congress that passage of the resolutions would adversely affect the war effort and they were withdrawn. Jewish sentiment was appeased by a statement which Rabbi Stephen S. Wise and Rabbi Abba Hillel Silver of the Zionist Organization of America were authorized by President Roosevelt to make, to the effect that the United States had never given its approval

---

[13] Crum, *Behind the Silken Curtain*, p. 36-37. A number of statements are attributed to the present author which are completely apocryphal.

to the 1939 White Paper. When the Arab leaders protested this, the President sent them a message saying that while it was true we had never approved the White Paper it was equally true that we had never taken any position with respect to it!

By this time the pressure on the United States administration to come out strongly in favor of the Zionist position was becoming intense. It must be borne in mind that the basic element in the average American citizen's attitude toward the Middle East, and toward Palestine in particular, was one of ignorance, and a vague recollection that the Bible spoke of the return of the Jews to Zion. Americans are by nature influenced by humanitarian motives, and our concern for the plight of the Jews in Europe was very real. These factors, plus the unremitting pressure exerted by the Zionists on all public officials and on the public at large, made it almost inevitable that our policy in this period should tend more and more to favor the Zionist point of view, ending with our official endorsement of a Jewish state.[14] It is ironic that this crystallization of our policy toward the Jewish side in the dispute came at the same time as our interests in the Arab world were coming into sharper focus because of wartime developments in the area. These included our participation in the wartime Middle East Supply Center, the enhanced importance to us of strategic factors resulting from our emergence as a global power, and the greatly increased exploitation of Middle Eastern oil. Thus the pull between our conflicting interests became stronger.

After the end of the war in Europe, President Truman sent Earl Harrison, the American representative on the Inter-governmental Committee on Refugees, to Europe to survey the situation of the Jewish survivors in the displaced persons' camps. Harrison reported[15] that the vast majority of the stateless Jews in the camps wanted to go to Palestine. He urged that 100,000 of them be permitted to do so at once (this figure had been suggested by the Jewish Agency).

In August 1945 the President forwarded the Harrison report to Prime Minister Clement Attlee of Great Britain, endorsing the proposal that 100,000 Jewish persons be admitted to Palestine. His letter arrived when the British government was debating what do to about the Palestine question, as it was obvious that with the end of the war it was necessary to make some decisions. Attlee seized upon the President's message to respond with a proposal that the two governments

---

[14] See, in this general context, Safran, *The United States and Israel*; Khouri, *op. cit.*; the *Memoirs* of Harry S Truman; *The Forrestal Diaries*; and Dean Acheson's memoirs.

[15] The Harrison Report may be found in Hurewitz.

should set up a joint body to examine the situation of the Jews in Europe and the Palestine question. This led to the appointment of the Anglo-American Committee of Inquiry, which spent some four months examining the situation in Europe and the Middle East in early 1946 and of which I became secretary.

The Anglo-American Committee of Inquiry, the seventeenth of the eighteen commissions appointed to study the Palestine question, consisted of six American and six British members, chosen on the basis of having had no previous experience with Palestine (see appendix E). The Committee first held hearings in Washington and then went to London for further hearings. During our stay in London, we met with Foreign Secretary Ernest Bevin, who assured the members of the Committee that if they came back with a unanimous report he would do all in his power to carry it out, a remark which made a profound impression on the members and which was very much in their minds when they were writing their report.

The Committee split into subcommittees to visit the various areas in Europe where there were Jewish displaced persons, and then proceeded to Cairo for more hearings. Early in March the Committee arrived in Jerusalem and spent the rest of the month in Palestine.

At this period, the security situation in Palestine dominated everyone's life. The country was an armed camp and the principal British officials travelled about with jeeps fore and aft containing plainclothesmen with tommy guns. The offices which we were provided by the government of Palestine were surrounded by barbed wire and guards. This was because Jewish terrorism was at a peak. This activity was most difficult for the authorities to combat, because there was a wide measure of sympathy for the terrorists throughout the Jewish community and because the British were understandably reluctant to adopt a policy of harsh reprisals, as they were to do, for example, in the Malay Peninsula or in Kenya, against people who had just been through the horrors of the Holocaust.

Soon after the Committee's arrival, the British High Commissioner gave a reception in its honor at Government House (later to become UN headquarters). The gulf between the Arab and Jewish communities became immediately apparent, since the Arabs boycotted the reception, not wishing to be associated with the Jewish invited guests. This pattern was to be a feature of the Palestine scene wherever we went, and all activities had to be organized with Jews and Arabs separately, never together.

The Committee's hearings in Jerusalem were featured by the appearance of Dr. Weizmann (later to be Israel's first President), who made a deep impression with his powerful personality, his well reasoned presentation, and his close physical resemblance to Lenin. Other Jewish leaders who were heard were David Ben Gurion, Golda Meir and David Horowitz for the Jewish Agency and Dr. Judah Magnes for the *Ihud* group which stressed cooperation with the Arabs. The Arab case was presented by Jamal Husayni and Awni Abd al-Hadi, who put forward a rigid, unimaginative line of argument, reiterating that Palestine was Arab and the Jews were interlopers. Their performance suffered in comparison with the highly articulate presentation by a young Arab intellectual, Albert Hourani who, along with Weizmann, made the greatest impression on the Committee. The witnesses also included a number of British civil and military officials and ecclesiastical figures, Christian, Muslim and Jewish, who gave some insight into the complexities of the religious issue. The Committee then broke again into subcommittees with some members visiting neighboring Arab capitals and some staying in Palestine to continue their investigations into the economic and social spheres. At the end of the month we proceeded to Lausanne, Switzerland, where the members settled down to write their report.

The important thing to bear in mind with regard to the report of the Anglo-American Committee of Inquiry (which was submitted to the two governments under date of April 20, 1946) is that the Committee's ten carefully worded recommendations were intended to be integral parts of a single whole, with concessions to one side balanced against concessions to the other. The last thing the members anticipated was that one or two of the recommendations would be accepted and not the entire report.

Thus, a recommendation that 100,000 Jewish displaced persons be admitted immediately to Palestine was balanced by an assertion that Palestine could not absorb all the homeless Jews and by recommendations designed to raise the standard of living of the Arab population and especially to improve Arab education. The Committee sought to resolve the conflicting Arab and Jewish claims to the country by declaring that Palestine should be neither an Arab nor a Jewish state. Just what the members had in mind for the future political structure of the country is nowhere stated in the report, although partition was explicitly rejected. It seems clear, however, that the members were thinking in terms of a bi-national state. Here they were in error, as by 1946 it was too late for this kind of solution.

In any event, neither the British nor the American governments accepted the Committee's report. President Truman issued a statement saying he welcomed the recommendation respecting the 100,000 Jews and one or two additional provisions but would have to take other parts of the report under advisement. Prime Minister Attlee said that the British government would have to consult the United States about the extent of assistance (particularly in the military sphere) it would be prepared to offer before deciding what action to take. Neither Arabs nor Jews were pleased with the report. The fact that the report was not implemented, however, should not obscure the fact that it is still of interest as an analysis of conflicting attitudes and as an effort by men of good will to find a reasonable and moderate solution.

In the summer of 1946, an American delegation went to London for discussions with the British covering the whole range of subjects examined by the Anglo-American Committee of Inquiry, including the comments on the report submitted to the British government by the Arabs and Jews under the "full consultation" formula. From these discussions emerged a proposal (known as the Morrison-Grady plan after Herbert Morrison and Henry F. Grady, the heads of the British and American delegations) for provincial autonomy, that is, for converting Palestine into a Jewish province, an Arab province and an area, including Jerusalem, under British trusteeship.[16] The two provinces would have control over their own local affairs, and the scheme was so devised as to be capable of evolving toward a unitary, bi-national state or toward partition. The immediate admittance of 100,000 Jews was foreseen. While the British government announced its support for the Morrison-Grady plan, President Truman stated that the United States could not go along with it. Neither the Arabs nor the Jews accepted the plan, and the British invited representative Arabs and Jews to a conference in London.

The Jewish Agency now put forward a proposal for partition and for "a viable Jewish state in an adequate area" of Palestine. This proposal was endorsed by President Truman. In a statement issued on the eve of Yom Kippur in October, he again called for the immediate admission of 100,000 Jews to Palestine. At this time, an important election was pending in New York, and Governor Thomas E. Dewey,

---

[16] A summary of the Morrison-Grady proposals is given in *The Political History of Palestine* . . . and Khouri.

leader of the Republican Party, countered with a call for the admission of "not 100,000 but several hundred thousand Jews."[17]

At the London conference, the Arabs proposed that Palestine should become an independent Arab state and that the control over Jewish immigration should be in Arab hands. The British made a counterproposal (known as the "Bevin scheme") for a five-year trusteeship, with substantial autonomy for Arab and Jewish areas, or cantons. When this was rejected by both parties, the British Foreign Secretary announced (February 18, 1947) that it had decided to submit the whole matter to the United Nations, since no agreement could be reached with the Arabs and Jews.

While the British have been criticized for thus appearing to wash their hands of the Palestine problem, it must be conceded that their exasperation was understandable. The security situation in Palestine itself was deteriorating steadily, with widespread Jewish terrorism greatly adding to the thankless task of the administration. There were repeated incidents where British officers and men and civilians were kidnapped, flogged, and even put to death, leading to corresponding reprisals. Illegal immigration continued. On top of this, throughout this period there was a very real feeling of annoyance in high British quarters at the American disposition to intervene in the problem without showing a willingness to undertake any responsibility of a military character.

At all events, a special session of the United Nations General Assembly met in April 1947 and set up a commission (the United Nations Special Committee on Palestine, or UNSCOP) which was the eighteenth and last of the Palestine inquiry commissions. This body submitted a majority and a minority report for consideration by the General Assembly in the autumn. The majority report,[18] which took as its basis the assumption that Jewish and Arab claims were irreconcilable, proposed the partition of the country. There would be a Jewish state and an Arab state in economic union with each other, and an area surrounding Jerusalem would be placed under United Nations administration. It was widely reported that several members of the majority were sympathetic to the Zionist point of view. The minority report proposed an independent federal state.

---

[17] For developments throughout the period, see *Supplementary Memorandum by the Government of Palestine, including notes on evidence given to the United Nations Special Committee on Palestine up to the 12th July, 1947.*

[18] United Nations Special Committee on Palestine, *Report to the General Assembly*, Lake Success, 1947.

The task of drawing viable boundaries for a Jewish state was complicated by the fact that at the time the population of the country comprised some 1,200,000 Arabs and 650,000 Jews. Even though the Jewish inhabitants were largely concentrated in certain areas such as the coastal plain, it was hard to devise a Jewish state that made any sense without incorporating large numbers of Arabs in it, and the boundaries suggested for the Arab state were gerrymandered to say the least. The distribution of population as recommended in the UNSCOP majority report was as follows:

	Jews	Arabs	Total
Jewish state	498,000	407,000	905,000[19]
Arab state	10,000	725,000	735,000
Jerusalem	142,000	68,000	210,000
Total	650,000	1,200,000	1,850,000

When the majority report was made public, the Zionists gave it their reluctant approval, while the Arabs came out strongly against it. In the General Assembly, the United States backed the proposal strongly and worked hard behind the scenes to bring about its adoption. Partition was also supported by the Soviet Union. On November 29, 1947, the majority plan, with some modifications, was approved by the Assembly by a vote of 33 to 13, with 10 abstentions.[20] The British were among those abstaining. Between the vote in committee (when an actual minority of those voting had been in favor of the plan) and the final vote in the Assembly, several delegations switched their votes to support partition, as a result of arm twisting by the United States delegation. Previously the Arabs had been defeated by one vote in committee on a motion[21] to ask the International Court of Justice at The Hague for an advisory opinion as to whether the General Assembly had the power to partition Palestine against the wishes of the majority of its inhabitants (it should be noted in any event that the partition resolution was worded merely as a recommendation to the Mandatory Power to adopt the majority report of UNSCOP). The question as to

---

[19] The figures proposed for the Jewish state need to be modified by the revealing statement in the report that "in addition there will be in the Jewish state about 90,000 Beduins, cultivators and stock-owners who seek grazing further afield in dry seasons." In other words, as these additional 90,000 persons could hardly be Jews, the Arab population of the Jewish state would total 497,000, as compared with 498,000 Jews— a very slim majority indeed.

[20] United Nations, General Assembly, Resolution No. 181 (II) of November 29, 1947, Partition of Palestine.

[21] Khouri, op. cit.

whether this was within the Assembly's competence has never been decided.

The security situation in Palestine grew worse, with increased terrorist activity and with the outbreak of actual fighting between Arabs and Jews. The United Nations Palestine Commission, which had been set up by the November 29 resolution of the General Assembly, reported to the Secretary General that an international police force would be necessary to implement partition. Such a force, however, was not established. At a meeting of the Security Council in March 1948 the United States announced that it was withdrawing support for partition, having concluded that it could not be carried out peacefully. We urged that Palestine be placed under a temporary UN trusteeship.

Events, however, were moving too fast for this. While the United Nations continued to grapple unsuccessfully with the problem, the British continued to make plans for their withdrawal from Palestine (scheduled for mid-May), the Jews continued to make plans for setting up their state at that time, and the Arabs continued to make plans for opposing this by force. All these contingencies duly came to pass.

As the ship bearing the last British High Commissioner sailed from Haifa port late on May 14, 1948, leaders of the Jewish community, who had laid careful plans for this day, met in Tel Aviv and proclaimed the state of Israel. The new state was recognized by President Truman within minutes of its creation. Simultaneously Arab forces from Egypt, Trans-Jordan, Iraq, Syria and Lebanon, some of which were already in Palestine, advanced and engaged in fighting with Jewish forces. It was then that the majority of the Arab refugees left, creating the Arab refugee problem. The situation was highly confused and it is impossible to this day to say with certainty whether, as has been alleged by one side, they left because the Jews urged them to or, as has been alleged by the other side, because their own leaders urged them to. It is likely that each version is partially true and that many people simply panicked. At all events, many thousands left (the best estimates run around 700,000 to 800,000—the UN Economic Survey Mission in 1949, for example, said about 726,000). Eventually most of them came under the care of the United Nations.

Arab disorganization and lack of planning contrasted, as in the June War, with Jewish efficiency. In the fighting the Arabs soon discovered that they had been overconfident. The Israelis fought well and bitterly. The Security Council ordered a cease-fire and the United Nations Mediator, Count Folke Bernadotte of Sweden, managed to secure agreement on this for a short period in June. During the brief cease-fire the Israelis obtained considerable quantities of military equipment from Czechoslovakia and other countries. When fighting resumed in July, the Israelis started to push the Arabs back and took considerable territory beyond what they would have had under the United Nations partition plan, in Galilee, in the center of the country, and in the south. They also secured and held after bitter fighting a corridor to Jerusalem. The city itself was occupied partly by them and partly by the Arabs.

Count Bernadotte was assassinated by Jewish terrorists in Jerusalem in September 1948 and Dr. Ralph Bunche became acting Mediator. Fighting continued and early in the next year the Egyptians, whose forces had been pretty well mauled (witness the account of a young Egyptian officer named Jamal Abd al-Nasir) sued for an armistice. The other Arab states followed suit. Dr. Bunche met with Israeli and Arab representatives on the Island of Rhodes where he skillfully conducted long and difficult negotiations which finally culminated in the Armistice Agreements of 1949 between Israel and its four Arab neighbors—Egypt, Syria, Lebanon and Jordan. Iraq, which had participated in the war and held a portion of the front, was represented by Jordan. These agreements[22] were admittedly not perfect but it was no mean achievement to have obtained them at all, especially as the Arabs were bitter and disillusioned after their defeat, and reluctant to have anything to do with Israel.

The Armistice settlement did not provide a solution for Jerusalem, which continued to be divided between Israel and Jordan with the cease-fire line running through the city. An account of the different proposals advanced for the internationalization of the city is given in appendix F. This whole subject is a highly recondite one, with which few people are familiar. In fact, I am reminded of the remark attributed to Lord Palmerson regarding the Schlesvig-Holstein problem. He is said to have commented that there were only three persons who had understood this problem: the Prince Consort, who was dead; a university professor, who had gone mad; and himself—and he had quite forgotten it.

---

[22] The texts of the Armistice Agreements were published in 1949 by the United Nations Security Council, as: United Nations Security Council, 4th Year, Special Supplement No. 1 (Jordan-Israel), No. 2 (Syria-Israel), No. 3 (Egypt-Israel), and No. 4 (Lebanon-Israel). The text of the Egypt-Israel Agreement may also be found in Hurewitz, and extracts from this agreement are given in Burns, *Between Arab and Israeli*. Khouri gives extracts from the agreements with Jordan and Syria and Gervasi, *op. cit.*, extracts from the Jordanian agreement. See Chapter V.

At all events, it will suffice here to point out that in 1948 and 1949 the General Assembly of the United Nations passed resolutions reaffirming support for the concept of an international city under the UN but the next year, 1950, the Assembly failed to agree on any plan for internationalization and there the matter was allowed to rest for seventeen years. Meanwhile the United Nations, and the Great Powers, including the United States, continued to consider Jerusalem to be an international city and were tacitly permitted to do so by the two occupying powers, Israel and Jordan.

In the early years after the Armistice Agreements there emerged the pattern that was to dominate the course of Arab-Jewish relationships for the next 18 years—tension along the Armistice lines, occasional shooting incidents, sabotage, raids, reprisals, sometimes actual warfare, with intervals of relative quiet. Soon after the successful conclusion of the Armistice Agreements, the United States was instrumental in getting the British and French governments to join with us in what became known as the Tripartite Declaration (May 25, 1950). This covered the supply of arms to the Arab states and Israel, in an effort to prevent an arms race, and also pledged the three signatory governments to take action, both within and outside the United Nations, in the event of any attempt by the states in question to violate frontiers or Armistice lines (see appendix G). The provisions of the Declaration with regard to the maintenance of a "certain level" of armed forces by the states involved were manifestly difficult of enforcement. In spite of this, the Tripartite Declaration remained the cornerstone of our Palestine policy until the mid-1950s when first the supply of arms in large quantities by the Soviet Union to Egypt and then the action of Great Britain and France in joining with Israel to attack Egypt rendered it a dead letter. Its guarantee of frontiers and Armistice lines, however, was repeated in later US government statements of policy, notably by President John F. Kennedy in May 1963 and President Lyndon B. Johnson in May and June 1967.

In the years after 1949, efforts were made on occasion by outside countries, including the United States, to bring about a settlement of the Arab-Israel dispute. However, these efforts always came up against the stumbling block that the positions of the two parties on the basic issues (refugees, Jordan waters, the Arab boycott, Jerusalem and so on) were so far apart as to be irreconcilable. That is to say, any proposals that would be acceptable to one side would not be acceptable to the other. The readiness of the American and British governments to assist in finding a solution was made clear during the year 1955 in major foreign policy speeches by Secretary of State John Foster Dulles and Foreign Secretary Anthony Eden, respectively. Dulles said that the United States was prepared to offer financial aid and a guarantee of borders if that would help, and that as a part of the examination of the different aspects of the problem we would favor a United Nations review of the status of Jerusalem.[23]

Earlier, beginning in 1953, the late Eric Johnston had gone out to the Middle East, with the backing of the United States, to try to gain the assent of Israel and the Arab states to the Unified Development Plan for the water resources of the Jordan Valley. This plan was not accepted by either side, although in later years both Israel and Jordan began unilaterally to implement some of its provisions. It is still considered to contain the elements of the best solution of the waters problem (see appendix H).

Efforts toward a settlement were put back by the decision of Egypt to accept Soviet bloc arms, already mentioned, and by the nationalization of the Suez Canal Company. Two international conferences were held in London in August and September 1956 in an effort to find a solution to the problem of the Canal but these did not lead to a settlement and in October of that year Israel, with the support of Great Britain and France, attacked Egypt. David Ben Gurion, Prime Minister of Israel at the time, has stated that his country acted because the activities of the guerrillas sent over the line from Egypt made Israel's position unbearable. There was also a deep feeling of frustration in Israel at Egypt's continuing refusal to allow Israel the use of the Suez Canal. More than thirteen years after the event, British and French motivations are still being argued about but it seems clear that the action brought little gain to those countries. They failed to topple Nasir and they became embroiled with their ally the United States, while the effect on their position in the Arab world was disastrous.

The United States took a strong line in the United Nations against the action of the British, French and Israelis and for a while this brought us some improvement in our relations with the Arab world. It also put considerable strain on our relations with Israel, especially when we had to apply economic pressure to obtain Israel's withdrawal from the Sinai Peninsula. A United Nations Emergency Force, with more authority than the Truce Supervision Organization operating under the Armistice Agreements, was deployed along the Egyptian side of the Armistice line (Israel refused to allow the force to enter its

---

[23] The text of Dulles' address is in Hurewitz.

territory) and at the mouth of the Gulf of Aqaba. It remained until 1967 when it was abruptly withdrawn at Nasir's instance.

The next few years were not marked by any outside initiatives looking toward a solution until in 1961 the United States proposed that the Palestine Conciliation Commission should send Dr. Joseph E. Johnson of the Carnegie Endowment out to the area to discuss with the parties certain proposals looking to a solution of the problem of the refugees. Our government was especially anxious to see a solution in view of the fact that for many years we had been contributing some 70 per cent of the funds for the United Nations agency dealing with the refugees, the United Nations Relief and Works Agency for Palestine Refugees in the Near East, or UNRWA. Dr. Johnson, like Eric Johnston, was not successful in his mission, but his proposals, like Eric Johnston's, are regarded as the best approach to date to a solution of an important element of the overall problem (see appendix I).

After the Suez War, the pattern of no-war, no-peace along the Armistice lines was resumed, with occasional flare-ups. There was no improvement in the basic issues outstanding between Israel and its Arab neighbors. The implacable Arab hostility toward Israel and the utter refusal to recognize its existence continued. Along the Syrian-Israel line, there were frequent incidents, with the Syrians at times shelling the border *kibbutzim* from the heights above and with each side provoking the other into cultivation disputes in the Demilitarized Zone. Border settlers came to be accustomed to sending their women and children into the shelters during these attacks, the threat of which was finally removed during the June War. Meanwhile, in the words of the Prophet Nehemiah (IV, 17): "Everyone with one of his hands wrought in the work, and with the other hand held a weapon."

There was a general feeling of frustration on both sides at the failure to achieve any kind of settlement and at the need to divert to military expenditure resources which could have gone into economic development. The development at the Arab summit meetings of the Palestine Liberation Movement and its constant propaganda to the effect that Israel must be destroyed raised passions on the Arab side and caused great anxiety in Israel. And the Arab refugees continued to eke out a living in their camps and to be a financial burden on the international community.

By way of summarizing United States government policy toward the Arab-Israel problem in the years leading up to the 1967 crisis, it can be said that our policy was to favor peace, to support the efforts of the

United Nations in maintaining the cease-fire, and to try to prevent an arms race. We refrained in general from taking an initiative toward a settlement but were always prepared to support any likely proposals that might come forward. The touch-stone of our official policy was even-handedness, an approach which could not have been avoided in view of the nature of the problem and the past history of our involvement in it, but which was extremely difficult to maintain in practice. The conflict between the attitudes of the parties was so complete, and their positions so intractable, however, that it is hard to see what else we could have done. Our government would certainly have been unlikely to have come out officially in favor of one party or the other. For example, had we decided to adopt a wholly pro-Israel policy, we could not have done so, because of our stake in the Arab world, and vice versa.

At the same time, while we in the government constantly referred to our policy as being one of even-handedness and impartiality, the overall American performance has created a totally different impression in the Middle East. It has become axiomatic that anyone running for office in the United States feels compelled for political reasons to affirm support for Israel and to speak as if we had some particular security commitment calling upon us to supply Israel with arms, which we do not. There is also the fact of large-scale public and private American aid to Israel—$1 billion to public funds since 1948, with private contributions (tax-exempt as charitable donations) running around $200 million per year and with $120,000,000 raised in ten days during the 1967 crisis. In these circumstances, no matter what we tell the Arabs, they remain completely unconvinced that we are being impartial, and in fact we are not. This of course tends to make them look to the USSR for support.

A final comment that might be made regarding our policy is that the position of constantly being in the middle was completely unwelcome to the two parties to the dispute. Both sides were unhappy, wanting our wholehearted support for their own point of view. Both, for example, wanted us to supply more arms than we thought we should do (our approach has continued to be that of seeking not to be a major supplier of arms and equipment to either side, although there have been a few exceptions). The Israelis, seeking a specific security guarantee, were disappointed not to get it. The Arabs, feeling betrayed since the First World War and especially since 1948, inevitably regarded us as pro-Israeli. Each side kept urging us to be "fair," that is to support its position.

Those of us in the field who were dealing with the problem from day to day were constantly aware not only of the complexities of our position but also of its frustrations. In fact we felt every sympathy with the comment of one of the early British administrators in Palestine, Sir Ronald Storrs, that "two hours of Arab grievances drive me into the synagogue while after an intensive course of Zionist propaganda I am prepared to embrace Islam."[24]

[24] The *Memoirs* of Sir Ronald Storrs, p. 358.

V

The Role of the United Nations

An important result of the Armistice settlement of 1949 was a continuing United Nations presence in Jerusalem and all along the borders between Israel and its Arab neighbors. It is therefore essential, in seeking to understand the situation as it has existed over the past twenty years, to have some knowledge of the nature of the Armistice Agreements and of the terms of reference of UNTSO—the United Nations Truce Supervision Organization, with headquarters in Jerusalem.[1]

The Armistice Agreements, as their texts explicitly state, were intended to be temporary only. It was expected when they were negotiated at Rhodes that it would not be long before they were replaced by a permanent peace. In fact, each agreement begins with the words: "With a view to promoting the return of permanent peace in Palestine . . ." and goes on ". . . the establishment of an armistice between the armed forces of the two parties is accepted as an indispensable step toward the liquidation of armed conflict and the restoration of peace . . ." The parties agreed not to resort to force or to commit or threaten military aggression. It was also agreed between the parties that nothing in the Armistice Agreements would in any way prejudice their rights, claims or positions in any eventual peaceful settlement. Changes in the Agreements could be made by consent of both parties but neither one could unilaterally free itself from its Armistice obligations. Each Agreement provided for the establishment of a Mixed Armistice Commission composed of an equal number of representatives from each side with a UN chairman.

---

[1] For the texts of the Armistice Agreements, see the sources listed in Chapter IV. For general background on the Agreements and on UNTSO, see Burns, *Between Arab and Israeli;* Hutchison, *Violent Truce;* and von Horn, *Soldiering for Peace;* also "An UNTSO Executive's View" by Byron V. Leary in *Mid East,* published by the Americans Friends of the Middle East, Washington, September 1968, special issue on Jerusalem. All four of these writers served with UNTSO, two of them (Burns and von Horn) as Chief of Staff. See also Khouri, *The Arab-Israel Dilemma,* Chapter VII.

No attempt was made at Rhodes to foresee every contingency that might arise or to set up procedures for dealing with every matter at issue between the parties. The emphasis was getting a reaffirmation of the cease-fire.

The Armistice lines, which had been drawn on the basis of existing military positions, were never intended to be a permanent border. In many places they made no sense, dividing villages from their lands and creating impossible defensive positions. Nor was it ever thought that the agreements themselves would over a period of years be subjected to needless and for the most part sterile haggling between the parties, with the UN often powerless to take effective action. The wonder is, in the circumstances, that the Armistice machinery worked so well. It did provide a forum for the airing of disputes and a means of relieving tension, although manifestly it failed twice—in 1956 and 1967—to prevent war.

In August 1949 the Security Council assigned to UNTSO the dual task of maintaining the unconditional cease-fire (by reaffirming the "order" for a cease-fire in Palestine contained in its basic resolution of July 15, 1948) and of assisting the parties in the supervision and observance of the Armistice Agreements. Accordingly UNTSO provided the Mixed Armistice Commissions, with their Chairmen and military observers who were stationed at certain points along the Armistice lines and elsewhere throughout the area.

The main thing to bear in mind in connection with the work of UNTSO is that it could obtain results only with the cooperation of the parties. While it could and did take the initiative in reestablishing the cease-fire when it broke down, as it often did, the Mixed Armistice Commissions could investigate and take decisions only with the consent of the parties. Their observers, who were not armed, could go only where each party said they could go. Their "decisions" were more in the nature of advisory opinions than judicial rulings. Neither the Chief of Staff of UNTSO nor the Armistice Commissions had the means of enforcing their decisions. The Chief did have the ultimate independent recourse of reporting to the Security Council on the observance of the cease-fire and often was requested by the Security Council to report on a complaint placed before it by one of the parties. The UNTSO Chairmen of the Mixed Armistice Commissions, however, were limited, when the latter had ceased to meet regularly, to making representations and recommendations for relieving existing tensions and for the observance of provisions of the Armistice Agreements on the basis of such observation and investigation by UNTSO observers as circumstances permitted.

The matters with which UNTSO dealt ranged from returning cattle which had strayed across the line to coping with a serious breach of the cease-fire. The work of the observers was tedious, often hazardous (twenty-two UN personnel have died in the performance of their duties in the Palestine area), and unrewarding. Both parties tended to resent the presence of the UN, whose representatives were caught in the middle much as were the members of the Consular Corps and who led the same schizophrenic existence. We often used to compare notes and were in agreement that if any of us said anything that could be taken to indicate sympathy with one side in the dispute, the other side would immediately accuse us of partiality. The frustrations of the UN observers were enhanced by the limitations under which they had to operate and by the often provocative positions adopted by the parties.

UNTSO had to deal with numerous instances of sabotage from across the various Armistice lines into Israeli territory. These might involve minor damage to a pump or water line or they might result in loss of life. To the limited extent permitted by the parties, the UN would hold an investigation, interview witnesses, and try to ascertain the facts, regarding which there would always be two diametrically opposed versions. The work of the observers was hampered by the fact that they did not have their own interpreters but had to rely on those provided by the parties (which allowed for the possibility of coaching witnesses). Nor did the UN have its own tracking dogs. When it came to a question of tracking down the perpetrators of a given incident, the UN observers had to depend upon the services of dogs provided first by one party and then by the other. At the demarcation line the observers actually had to go through what was called the "handover" of footprints, that is, the transfer of the scent from one dog to the other. These procedures were cumbersome and inefficient to say the least, and it is no wonder that the UN investigation often failed to produce concrete evidence or lead to a definitive finding.

It might be noted here that there was a difference between the terms of reference of UNTSO and those of UNEF, the United Nations Emergency Force deployed along the Israeli-Egyptian border after the Sinai war. UNEF observers were allowed to carry arms and to detain infiltrators. Even so, they were not permitted by Israel to be stationed on the Israeli side of the line, either when UNEF was set up in 1957 or in May 1967, when Nasir requested its withdrawal from

Egyptian territory and the UN Secretary General again asked Israel to let UNEF come onto its side. Incidentally, the alacrity with which the Secretary General complied with Nasir's request serves to underline the point that the consent of the parties is essential to the maintenance of a United Nations presence in the area.

In the years following the conclusion of the Armistice Agreements, as it became evident that peace was not soon to be achieved, there was considerable discussion of possible ways of strengthening the Armistice machinery. The conclusion always reached, however, was that this would require in the first place the renegotiation of the agreements themselves, which was hardly feasible, as well as the provision by UN headquarters of additional personnel and other resources. Given the perpetual shortness of funds of the world organization, this was simply not possible.

The success which UNTSO achieved in carrying out its responsibilities under the Armistice Agreements varied from country to country. The agreement which worked best was that between Israel and Lebanon, where there happened to be fewer problems at issue and where there was a fixed demarcation line corresponding precisely to the former frontier. The Jordanian Agreement gave rise to a host of problems, especially as the demarcation line between Israel and Jordan was the longest of the four, but in general worked fairly well. The Egyptian Armistice Agreement was unilaterally denounced by the Israelis in 1956, at the time of the Sinai campaign. Although this action was not accepted by either the UN or Egypt, and the Mixed Armistice Commission continued in a purely *pro forma* existence, the Agreement remained largely inactive. In actual practice contact was maintained between the parties through UNEF, which was largely successful in maintaining the cease-fire. The Syrian Agreement provided UNTSO with its thorniest problems, in later years at least, even though the Syrian-Israel demarcation line was the shortest of all. The disagreement between the parties became so sharp that the Israel-Syria Mixed Armistice Commission was unable to hold regular meetings after 1951. Only a very few emergency meetings took place in subsequent years.

In general, the four Armistice Agreements were identical, but with exceptions to cover the many situations peculiar to each. For example, the Israel-Egypt Agreement provided for a demilitarized zone around Al-Auja, the headquarters of the Mixed Armistice Commission, which was a strategic spot because it stood at the key highway junction on the interior road between Israel and the Sinai. It was occupied by Israel in

1955 and the last UN military observer stationed there was ousted by Israel in October 1956, both of which actions were in defiance of the United Nations.

The Egyptian Agreement, unlike the other three which prohibited all aggressive action conducted from territory controlled by one party against the other, limited such actions to military acts committed by land, sea or air forces. Because of this provision, one authority has suggested that Egypt's closing of the Suez Canal to Israeli shipping was a violation not of the letter of the Armistice Agreement but only of its spirit.[2]

The Agreement between Jordan and Israel contained a clause which was the cause of endless difficulty. This was Article 8, which provided for the appointment by the parties of a special committee to consider specific matters on which, in the words of the Agreement "agreement in principle already exists." It was specified that these matters included such items as free movement of traffic on certain roads, resumption of the normal functioning of the cultural and humanitarian institutions on Mount Scopus (i.e. Hadassah Hospital and the Hebrew University) and access thereto, free access to the Holy Places and cultural institutions (meaning Jewish) and use of the cemetery (Jewish) on the Mount of Olives, provision of water and electricity for the Old City and resumption of operation of the railroad to Jerusalem. In the event, however, the Special Committee did not meet after 1949 and settled only the matter of the railroad. The assumption that there was agreement on the other points was certainly not borne out, owing largely to Jordanian intransigence and desire to maintain the status quo for security reasons. Denial of access to the Wailing Wall in the Old City was, as the years passed, the single most constant and most bitter Israeli complaint.

The Israel-Syria Agreement also contained a provision which gave rise to endless trouble. This was with respect to the Demilitarized Zone that was set up, in three sections, along much of the former boundary between Palestine and Syria. The reason for this was that when the fighting stopped there were units of Syrian troops in occupation of certain territory west of this boundary. To secure the evacuation of these areas by the Syrians, a device was hit upon (the inspiration for this is generally believed to have come from Ralph Bunche) to demilitarize these areas so that no armed forces (except locally recruited police) would be permitted and only normal civilian activities allowed. The Chairman of the Mixed Armistice Commission was made respon-

---

[2] Azcárate, Mission in Palestine, p. 120.

sible for the implementation of these provisions but without any administrative authority. The provisions proved impossible to enforce, since Israel denied the competence of the Chairman and claimed sovereignty over the Demilitarized Zone. Both parties repeatedly and steadily encroached upon the zone, especially Israel, a process which eventually deprived Arab farmers of most of the cultivated land and led to Israel's control over practically the entire Demilitarized Zone.

In the early years after the Armistice settlement, there unfortunately occurred some erosion of the authority of the United Nations, largely because the inexperience of the UN administrators was no match for the determination of the parties to bring about certain changes in the ground rules. An example already mentioned is that of the Israeli take-over of the demilitarized zone at Al-Auja. The Chief of Staff of UNTSO at the time (General E. L. M. Burns of Canada) admits in his memoirs that he was "naïve" in not seeing what the real intentions of the Israelis were.[3] This area, it must be noted, served as the jumping-off place for Israeli operations in the Sinai Peninsula in both 1956 and 1967.

Another instance was Mount Scopus, a hill which is of very great strategic importance locally because it dominates the access to Jerusalem by road from several directions. Prior to the conclusion of the Armistice Agreements, a special agreement had been negotiated by the UN in 1948 with the Arab and Jewish military commanders, providing for the demilitarization of the Mount Scopus area and placing it under UN protection. In separate areas, divided by a no-man's land, armed Arab and Jewish civilian police were to be placed on duty under the UN commander. The parties agreed that the entire area was not to be used as a base for military operations, and that since Mount Scopus was surrounded by Jordanian territory the UN would make arrangements for the supply of the Jewish police detachment and for its relief at periodic intervals, which was the origin of the Scopus convoy.

Nevertheless, it soon developed that the Israelis were bent on asserting complete control over their area on Scopus and even denying access to UN personnel, in spite of the fact that the agreement provided that the whole area should be under UN protection. The Jordanians claimed that the Israelis were fortifying the buildings of Hadassah and the University and were smuggling arms in during the bi-weekly convoys and that the so-called Israeli police were really

---

[3] Burns, *op. cit.*, p. 97.

Israeli soldiers. The UN encountered the greatest difficulty in seeking to establish whether there was any basis for these allegations.

Frequently UNTSO personnel were refused entry into the Jewish area, and efforts by four successive Chiefs of Staff to inspect the Jewish installations either were frustrated or were only partially successful. That the Israelis were in fact turning the area into a military base was confirmed after the June War, when the weapons and other military equipment that they had cached there over the years were revealed.[4]

The most striking incident regarding the Scopus convoy occurred in 1952 and is known as "The Incident of the Barrel."[5] It reveals the atmosphere in which the convoys actually were run and the impotence of the UN in matters of this sort. On June 4, 1952, during the routine check such as was always carried out by the UN on materials and men being taken up to Mount Scopus, a UN observer dropped a test rod into a barrel said to contain fuel oil and encountered a metal object. The chief UN observer ordered the barrel removed from the convoy, whereupon the Israelis (in contravention of the Armistice) moved soldiers into no-man's land (where the inspection was taking place) and demanded the return of the barrel, unopened. The Jordanians for their part demanded that the barrel be opened. Both sides had their rifles at the ready and it looked as though a serious clash would break out, when the situation was saved by a UN observer who placed his foot upon the barrel, declaring it to be under UN protection. It was agreed that the barrel would be taken into the adjoining Mixed Armistice Commission headquarters pending discussion.

Some days later, just before the UN was about to open the barrel in the presence of both parties, the MAC building was occupied by armed Israeli troops, who placed a lock on the door of the room containing the barrel and refused to allow the representatives of the UN to have access to it (at that time the MAC headquarters happened to be on the Israeli side). The Israeli government simply declared that the barrel had been removed from the convoy and was no longer of any concern to the UN. After tortuous negotiations, it was agreed that the Israeli soldiers would be withdrawn and that the barrel would be opened in the presence of the Israeli and Jordanian delegates to the Mixed Armistice Commission. The Chief of Staff of UNTSO personally tested the barrel with a rod and upon encountering what he described as an "extraneous object," returned the barrel to the Israelis

[4] *The New York Times,* June 21, 1967; see also Randolph and Winston Churchill, *The Six Day War,* p. 124.

[5] The incident is mentioned in Burns, p. 158, and is covered in detail in Hutchison, *op. cit.,* p. 20 ff.

without further inspection, to the dismay of the Jordanians. His reasoning was that the barrel could not be regarded as part of the convoy, since its contents were not in accord with the manifest submitted by the Israelis. This ruling naturally tended to encourage smuggling, since the Israelis could either take their chances on getting illicit materials past the inspection or, if detected, simply remove them from the convoy. One result of this incident was that the UN moved MAC headquarters into no-man's land, where it remained thereafter.

It should not be assumed that by citing these examples of Israeli violations I wish to imply that there were not also Arab violations. On the contrary, the Arabs showed over the years that they also were capable of ignoring provisions of the Armistice Agreements which they found unpalatable or of contravening specific sections. The failure of Jordan to implement Article 8 of the Israel-Jordan Armistice, notably the denial of access to the Wailing Wall and other Jewish Holy Places that was so resented by the Jews of the world, has already been noted. For their part, the Syrians occupied certain portions of the Demilitarized Zone, notably in the area of Al-Hamma, and fired repeatedly into the Demilitarized Zone in areas from which the Israelis had evicted the original Palestinian Arab cultivators. These Syrian activities, and the later adoption by the Syrian government in the period before the June War of a deliberate policy of supporting guerrilla raids and sabotage against Israeli settlements, did much to bring about the war.

In addition to witnessing an erosion of the authority of the UN, the early years after the Armistice saw the development of the pattern which was to remain a characteristic of the situation along the Armistice lines until the outbreak of the June War, and which has resumed since: raid followed by reprisal, Arab guerrilla activity followed by Israeli retaliation. The fact that the Israeli retaliatory raids were often condemned by the UN Security Council as violations of the Armistice Agreements (which they were), while the Arab sabotage and terrorist activities which had led the Israelis to take reprisals were often not likewise condemned by the Security Council, owing to the difficulty of proving complicity on the part of the Arab governments, did not endear the UN to the Israelis. This contributed to exacerbating the relations between the government of Israel and UNTSO, and to making the situation of the UN personnel on the spot more uncomfortable.

The representatives of the UN were made even more uncomfortable by the various personal pressures brought to bear on them by the two sides. UNTSO personnel, both military observers and civilians, could pass freely back and forth between the two sides. Inevitably they were approached by persons on one side or the other with requests to smuggle articles across the line and inevitably a few of the UN people yielded to this temptation. This led to blackmail and to attempts to obtain information about confidential UN matters. Incidents of this type occurred on both the Israeli and Arab sides and the offenders, admittedly few in number, had to be removed.

A variant of this kind of activitiy was the widely rumored and apparently substantiated use by the Israelis of attractive young women for intelligence purposes. It was claimed that it was the Israeli practice to release from further military service any girl soldier who had succeeded in compromising a member of the UN and acquiring useful information from him. The Israeli government of course denied the existence of any such activities when they were alleged by the former UNTSO Chief of Staff, General Carl von Horn, in his memoirs. It is of interest, however, to recall that on a visit to Gaza in 1966 I learned from the Commander of UNEF that his men, at least, were the object of a similar campaign of blandishment.

The demarcation line along which UNEF was deployed in the Gaza Strip was paralleled by a track on the Israeli side which was patrolled several times a day by Israeli military vehicles. I was told that the Israelis frequently included in these patrols girl soldiers who were from the various countries which made up UNEF (the Scandinavian countries, India, or Brazil, for example) and who, speaking the men's own language, would try to engage them in conversation and distract them from their guard duties. The commanding general had to issue very strict regulations in an attempt to keep his men from having any contact with the Israelis.

Members of UNTSO who had incurred the displeasure of the Israeli government often found that they were subject to what can only be described as harrassment. They were attacked in the Israeli press and radio and demands were made for their removal—which actually did happen on several occasions. At least two Chiefs of Staff of UNTSO, as well as other personnel, were required to travel with an Israeli guard, allegedly for their own protection, whenever they entered Israeli jurisdiction. Israeli officials seemed to have a way of making themselves unavailable in a crisis when it suited their purpose to do so. All in all, it was understandable that almost all of our acquaintance among the members of UNTSO chose to live on the Jordanian rather than the Israeli side of Jerusalem, even though most of them had embarked on their tour of duty with a predilection toward Israel.

Following my arrival in Jerusalem in 1964, I had an opportunity to gain familiarity with many of the problems being handled by UNTSO. In Jerusalem itself there were frequent incidents. The Jordanian and Israeli sectors were separated by a no-man's land stretching along the Armistice line throughout the city. At the time of the cease-fire, the boundaries of no-man's land had been established by drawing a line, or rather two lines, showing the limits of the areas held by the Arab or Jewish forces, as the case might be. As it happened, the map used was of so small a scale, and the grease pencil employed was so thick, that when projected on the ground the lines were actually as wide as thirty meters in some places and even sixty in a few places. This led to endless wrangles in an area as built up as the city of Jerusalem, not only because many buildings turned out to extend from one sector into no-man's land but also because it was impossible to get agreement as to what should be done about that portion of a given house that was "on the width of the line." This might appear to be a small point but it was argued with passion at meeting after meeting of the Mixed Armistice Commission.

In 1951 this problem had resulted in an agreement signed at a Mixed Armistice Commission meeting which recognized certain houses then illegally occupied as "allowed houses" for normal civilian life but stipulated that "no further houses in the Jerusalem no-man's land will be occupied without prior agreement of both parties." Over the years some of these houses were fortified and other houses at least partly "on the width of the line" were occupied and fortified, although the UN had tried to prevent this. Frequently one party or the other would complain that a certain house was being newly occupied by the other in violation of the *status quo* or was being fortified. We would hear shots being exchanged, and sometimes people were injured or killed. Protracted meetings of the Armistice Commission would be held and some sort of finding would generally emerge, but given the UN's lack of enforcement authority the same problems would arise again and again. No agreement could be reached for dividing no-man's land or for determining the limits of the sovereignty of the parties.

In the fall of 1966 there occurred in the outskirts of Jerusalem a sabotage incident which illustrated many of the problems with which the representatives of the United Nations had to deal. I visited the scene shortly after the incident had taken place, in a row of apartment houses on a hillside in the so-called Romena quarter of the New City.

This overlooked a deep valley through which ran the Armistice demarcation line and beyond which, in full sight, was the Jordanian village of Bayt Iksa. The hill was so steep at the point where the buildings had been erected that the outer edges of the buildings had to be supported by concrete pillars. Charges had been exploded under two of the houses, curiously enough not under the pillars, which would have caused the whole building to collapse, but on the inner side, next to the ground. Four persons had been wounded and there had been some damage to both buildings, but this was not extensive.

The Israelis contended that infiltrators coming from the village of Bayt Iksa had crossed the line at night, made their way up the hillside using a path through a narrow gully, placed their explosives, and returned the same way. The UN made an investigation, using both Israeli and Jordanian dogs, but could not produce any evidence of infiltration at the point alleged. Indeed the path the saboteurs were said to have employed looked to me to be so well worn that it would have been almost impossible to identify any particular tracks. The Mixed Armistice Commission rendered an inconclusive ruling and that was the end of the matter, except that it served greatly to increase the apprehension of the Israelis that an incident of this nature could have taken place so near to the heart of the city.

There were several peculiar things about this episode which troubled the representatives of UNTSO and myself when we discussed it. The peculiar placing of the explosive charges, almost as though with the intent of causing as little damage as possible, and the fact that the high anti-infiltration fence, which guarded the line at the spot where the perpetrators of the bombing were said to have crossed, showed no signs of having been tampered with, much less cut, were hard to explain. Some suspicious souls went so far as to suggest that the incident might have been a plant. While this was never seriously alleged, there are aspects of the incident which remain unresolved on this day.

It is remarkable how much UNTSO accomplished under the handicaps with which it had to work. At the same time, it must be recorded that the UN's inability to cope satisfactorily with border incidents was a contributing factor, in late 1966 and 1967, to increased sabotage and terrorism, with resultant Israeli reprisal raids, and to heightened tension all along the line. Suggestions were put forward for means of decreasing infiltration, including the use of electronic devices, but these were still under consideration when war came.

During this period there were recurring problems involving the cultivation of fields in the Israel-Syria Demilitarized Zone. Specifically, the cause was that Israeli farmers were allegedly working on Arab-owned lands or encroaching upon areas not previously cultivated. A more fundamental explanation was Syrian resentment at the fact that since the Armistice Israel had successfully extended its *de facto* control over most of the Demilitarized Zone, establishing *kibbutzim*, depriving Arab farmers of previously cultivated fields, and progressively extending the line of cultivation eastwards. In early 1967, General Bull, the Chief of Staff of UNTSO, made determined but unsuccessful efforts to resolve these cultivation issues, which involved, among other things, the use by Israeli farmers of armored tractors to enforce cultivation claims and frequent shooting attacks by Syrians on Israeli civilians and settlements. General Bull was unable, however, even to arrange for marking on the ground the limits of a *status quo* of cultivation which had some years previously been agreed to in principle by both Israel and Syria. The tension caused by these cultivation incidents was another contributing factor to the outbreak of the war.

The June War had the effect of greatly reducing the rôle of the UN, because of the treatment accorded UNTSO by the Israelis during the war and immediately after. The main instance of this was the expulsion of General Bull and his staff from UNTSO headquarters on the first day of the war, June 5, 1967, the details of which were related to me by the General that same evening.[6] As late as the morning of that day, General Bull had received categorical assurances from both Israel and Jordan that in the event of hostilities they would respect the inviolability of UNTSO headquarters, located in an area between the Armistice lines at Government House, of which the UN had been custodian since 1948. About noon, after firing had broken out in the Jerusalem area, Bull's deputy, Colonel Johnson of the US Marine Corps, received a telephone call from the Israeli Foreign Ministry saying Cairo radio had announced that Jordanian troops had occupied Government House and asking if this was true. After checking the extensive grounds, Colonel Johnson called back to say the report was incorrect. He put down the phone and looked out the window to see Jordanian soldiers entering the grounds.

The Jordanians never actually occupied Government House. General Bull went out and spoke to the commanding officer, pointing out that this was United Nations territory and demanding that the troops

[6] General Bull's expulsion is covered in several reports from the Secretary-General of the UN to the Security Council, notably S/PV 1347 and S/7930, June 5, 1967.

leave. Meanwhile Colonel Johnson got in touch by telephone with the Jordanian Delegate to the Mixed Armistice Commission, who interestingly enough appeared thunderstruck on being told that Jordanian troops were at Government House. The General was about to try to get through urgently by phone to Amman when Israeli forces attacked, and entered the grounds from their side, led by a column of tanks with guns firing. A brisk battle ensued for several hours, by which time the Israelis had occupied Government House itself, now somewhat damaged, and had driven the Jordanians out of the area. The Israelis insisted on entering the building, asserting that there were Arab snipers there (which General Bull assured them there were not). Grenades and shells exploded all around while Bull and his staff, and some UN wives and children who had sought refuge there, took to the floor.

The General was then told by the Israelis that the group would have to evacuate Government House and proceed at once to the Israeli sector. They were given ten minutes, later extended to twenty, to gather together their papers and possessions. Bull, who was the only one who actually lived at Government House, had lost a good many of his personal belongings as his apartment had caught fire twice. After the UN party, under fire, had made their way into the New City in such of their vehicles as remained mobile, they were met by an official of the Foreign Ministry who told them they would be lodged temporarily in a local hotel.

In my opinion, the attempt to take the Government House area was a serious miscalculation on the part of the Jordanians which did Jordan, and the United Nations, a great disservice. It was an open invitation to the Israelis to move in, and it provided the latter with an essential base of operation for any action to take the Old City.

The Jordanian action is difficult to explain on any rational grounds. Government House stands on one of the highest hills in the Jerusalem area, known as Jabal Mukkabir, the highest being Mount Scopus. The terrain is very steep to the north, east and south, while only to the west does it shelve away gradually. Thus the hill provides a considerable topographical obstacle to an invading force from the Jordanian side, while the opposite is true of the Israeli side. Moreover, in any attempt to encircle and capture the Old City an Israeli force would be greatly aided by possession of Jabal Mukkabir as well as Mount Scopus, as was soon to be demonstrated rather emphatically. It readily can be seen, therefore, that the Jordanian action was an exceedingly rash one, presumably undertaken, like the attack on Jerusalem itself, at UAR instigation and representing the only advance (if it can be called that) made by Jordanian forces during the entire war. That this action was in fact taken at the instance of the Egyptian commander in Amman emerges from King Husayn's book on the war.[7]

The ill-conceived Jordanian entry into the Government House area had two important consequences. Not only did it give the Israeli Army an excuse to seize a valuable tactical advantage but it also severely hampered UNTSO.

Deprived of its main base and of its communications, records and other equipment, UNTSO was forced to operate under great difficulties. This curtailment of its activities (just when, in view of the fighting that was going on, one would expect its services to be needed the most) was not the only problem. By moving General Bull and his staff to Israeli-held territory the Israelis in effect brought UNTSO under their control and gravely impaired its impartiality in the eyes of the Arabs.

Simultaneously, the Israelis occupied the headquarters of the Jordan-Israel Mixed Armistice Commission in the no-man's land near Mandelbaum Gate. The MAC to all intents and purposes ceased to function. It had already been unsuccessful on two occasions on the morning of June 5 in trying to bring about a cease-fire.

A day or two after the occupation of MAC house by the Israeli forces, Colonel Johnson visited it. He was halted at the gate of the building by armed Israeli soldiers, who were obviously reservists, inadequately instructed as to their duties and responsibilities. In spite of his pointing out that as Deputy Chief of Staff of UNTSO he had every right to enter the building, they surrounded him and with rifles cocked prevented him from moving. A little drama then ensued, in which the six-foot-six Marine Colonel, who has a most commanding presence, stared down his captors, with his wife, who had accompanied him, looking on from the sidelines. This lasted about twenty minutes until a senior Israeli officer came along and ordered the Colonel's release.

After months of negotiating, the UN eventually got back to Government House, although within a smaller perimeter than before (one-third of the original area) and with not all of its valuable equipment restored. From the tower of the New City YMCA, where they had soon moved from their hotel, the UN officers had seen, with binoculars, the removal by the Israelis of considerable portions of the nearly $4,000,000 worth of communications equipment maintained

---

[7] Husayn of Jordan, *My "War" With Israel*, p. 61.

by the UN at Government House, as well as vehicles and other items. For some time the UN representatives were denied access to Government House, as was I when I requested permission to go there later on. When they were allowed to visit Government House periodically, they could establish that equipment continued to be taken out, in spite of assurances from the highest quarters. Eventually the UN went back to a virtually empty headquarters, although some of the missing equipment was subsequently returned. This did not include personal effects stored there which had been looted or destroyed. By this time the rôle of UNTSO had become a much reduced one.

After the war, the Israelis denounced the three remaining Armistice Agreements (it will be recalled that they had refused to recognize the validity of the Egyptian Agreement for the previous ten years). They began to refer to General Bull not as the Chief of Staff of UNTSO but as the personal representative of Secretary General U Thant. For all practical purposes, UNTSO's activities were confined to observation of the cease-fire along the Suez Canal and the Golan Heights, with additional observers arranged for by the Secretary General.

The change in status of UNTSO was not recognized by the UN itself. The official Israeli view on the subject was restated in the Security Council on April 27, 1968, by the Israeli representative, Mr. Yosef Tekoah who said:[8] "The Armistice is no more because the Arabs have destroyed it. The relations between Israel and the Arab states are now founded upon and regulated by the cease-fire. . . ."

The official UN view was stated by U Thant in his *Annual Report for 1966-67*, as follows:

> There has been no indication either in the General Assembly or in the Security Council that the validity and applicability of the Armistice Agreements have been changed as a result of recent hostilities. The Agreements provide that by mutual consent the signatories can revise or suspend them. There is no provision in them for unilateral termination of their application. . . .

The impasse thus remains complete.

---

[8] S/PV 1416, April 27, 1968.

VI

Conflict, June 1967: Origins and Consequences

"When Nasir put his ban on the Strait of Tiran," as an Israeli rock and roll song had it, the Middle East crisis of 1967 began in earnest. In fact, however, the situation in Jerusalem and all along Israel's borders with its Arab neighbors had been critical ever since the Samu' raid of the previous November.

During the latter part of 1966 the pattern of violence across the Armistice lines was very perceptibly intensified. In October, two incidents in the Jerusalem area which the Israelis believed to have been carried out by commandos based in Syria gave rise to great anxiety in Israel. There were repeated acts of sabotage and shooting incidents along the Syrian border, which were stepped up after the signing in November of a mutual defense pact between Syria and the UAR. However, when the Security Council of the United Nations met at Israel's request to hear its charges against the Syrians, a resolution condemning Syria was vetoed by the USSR.

In the early hours of November 13, shortly after the mining of a patrol vehicle near the Jordanian border in which three Israeli soldiers were killed and six wounded, Israeli troops crossed into Jordanian territory in force and carried out a retaliatory raid on the village of Samu', south of Hebron. Four thousand Israeli troops participated in the action and for the first time in a raid of this sort tanks were used. Jordanian troops coming to the defense of the village were ambushed and suffered severe losses in men and equipment. The Israelis withdrew after four hours, leaving, by UN count, 18 Jordanians killed (civilian and military), 134 wounded and 127 buildings destroyed, including the village clinic, the school and a large number of private houses. The village mosque was damaged. The Israelis claimed that this action had been undertaken because the village had harbored infiltrators coming originally from Syria.

The Security Council unanimously condemned Israel for the raid but the damage was done as far as the internal situation in Jordan was concerned. King Husayn and his government were sharply criticized throughout the West Bank for having allowed the incident to take place, and the Palestinians grew ever more restive. Rioting broke out in the Old City of Jerusalem and other West Bank towns, notably Nablus. For weeks there was an armed guard posted at our Old City Consulate, since the authorities were fearful that popular indignation would be diverted against the United States. Actually, a bomb was thrown into our garden but fortunately it was discovered before it went off. While things gradually quieted down to some extent, complete internal stability had not been restored by the time the real crisis erupted in May. Moreover, the Jordanians resented the fact that neither Egypt nor Syria had come to their aid.

Shortly after the Samu' raid, we had another of our schizophrenic experiences. One evening we went to dinner in Bethlehem where several of our Jordanian doctor friends who had been called to Samu' to take care of the wounded gave us some graphic first hand accounts of the incident: how a border guard heard the Israeli tanks assembling across the line before dawn and gave the alarm but it was not heeded; how the Jordanian soldiers, when they did arrive belatedly, failed to take cover on approaching the village and were thus sitting ducks for the Israeli guns; and how as a result of the complete ineptitude displayed by the authorities the people of the district were more angry with their own government than with Israel.

The next evening we dined in Tel Aviv with Israeli friends, who could not believe some of the things we told them about the extent of the destruction caused by their troops and who finally conceded that the raid had probably been a mistake.

There were serious shooting incidents in January 1967 and again in April, when the Syrians shelled three border *kibbutzim* in northern Israel. The Israelis sent in planes to silence the guns and a dogfight ensued in which the Syrians lost six fighter planes within an hour. Just afterwards we were in the area and visited one of the settlements which had been shelled—Gadot, near Huleh. The destruction of buildings was extensive and we spoke to some of the women who with their children had been in the shelters and so had escaped injury. Incidents of this kind were shocking and were a major cause of rising Israeli anger and frustration. Again, Nasir failed to come to the aid of a brother Arab.

By May the atmosphere along the Armistice lines had become so strained that it was clear something had to give. We did not see how the condition of no-war no-peace could continue much longer. Some Israelis even began to ask themselves whether it was a question of now or never, before Soviet arms made the Arabs stronger. One observer has described[1] the spring crisis of 1967 as a "textbook case," of the way in which tension rose steadily, and the situation escalated out of hand, from one incident to another, with the constant obbligato of Arab radio and press propaganda insisting that Israel must be swept into the sea.

The immediate impetus for the crisis was provided by the start on May 15 of an Egyptian build-up in the Sinai Peninsula. Nasir himself told the world in his (anti-climactic) resignation speech after the war, that "it all started in Syria" when reports of an Israeli concentration of forces on the Syrian frontier which he had received from Soviet sources caused him to move troops into the Sinai as a gesture of solidarity with Syria. United Nations military observers, however, investigated these alleged Israeli actions and reported that they could see no evidence to support them.[2] The same finding was made by US service attachés in Tel Aviv.

This was a familiar experience. Time and again the attachés and the UN observers would be asked to make these investigations and time and again they would report in the negative. It may be conceded that in view of Israel's compact territory, and the high degree of mobility of its armed forces, any extensive advance deployment of troops was hardly necessary. In this particular case, however, no proof has ever been adduced of an Israeli concentration of forces against Syria. At the same time, it must be recorded that certain public statements at this juncture by Israeli leaders, notably Chief of Staff Rabin and Prime Minister Eshkol, were interpreted by the Arabs as indicating an aggressive intent. Coincidentally, the Israelis ordered a partial call-up on May 16, to counter the Egyptian move into Sinai. It seems pretty clear in retrospect that no one in Israel at that time expected war, but public opinion was getting restive. Twice in the past few months Nasir had not come to the aid of fellow Arabs when they became embroiled with Israel—could he afford to do so again?

The next move was a request by Nasir that UNEF be withdrawn, a request that was promptly honored by Secretary General U Thant of

---

[1] Laqueur, p. 71.

[2] Report by Secretary-General U Thant to the Security Council on the Middle East Crisis, May 20, 1967, in *A Select Chronology and Background Documents Relating to the Middle East*, Senate Committee on Foreign Relations. The Arab states were informed of the negative results of the investigation.

the United Nations. When Nasir moved from this to his declaration (May 22) that the Strait of Tiran (protected up to that time by UNEF) would be closed to Israeli shipping, the situation became really critical. The strait, leading to the Gulf of Aqaba and to Israel's port of Eilat, was a vital lifeline for Israel, even though the closing of the strait had implications that were more political than economic.

The effect in Israel was to cause the government to send Foreign Minister Abba Eban on an urgent mission to Paris, London and Washington and to set in motion the first pressures for a national government representing a broad political spectrum. In Jordan, the effect was to cause King Husayn to ask Saudi Arabia and Iraq for troops to help defend Jordan and to send General Amir Khammash, Chief of Staff of the Jordan Arab Army, to Cairo on urgent consultations. (The King did not request help from Syria at this time because his government had just broken relations with that country following the premature explosion at the border of a Syrian vehicle carrying explosives apparently designed to blow up the leaders of the Jordanian government.) Meanwhile the Arab propaganda offensive continued unslackened.

The effect of these events on the United States government was that it concentrated its energies on seeking a solution to the problem of free navigation through the Strait of Tiran. At the same time the evacuation of American citizens from the Middle East began. In Jerusalem we received instructions to warn all non-essential Americans to leave. We started to send our wives with children to a safe haven in Athens or Rome. The workload increased markedly in our offices in both sectors of the city and the remaining wives volunteered to help.

On May 26 Muhammad Hasanayn Haykal, editor of *Al-Ahram* in Cairo and generally regarded as spokesman for President Nasir, wrote that war was inevitable. Soon after, General Khammash returned to Amman from Cairo and reported to King Husayn that the Unified Arab Command, the defense organism of the Arab League, was proving of no value in the growing crisis. The King decided to go to Cairo himself to see Nasir and make coordinated plans for the confrontation with Israel that he was now sure was coming.

On May 30, King Husayn flew to Cairo and met with Nasir. They signed a pact of mutual defense under which the King agreed that in the event of hostilities the Jordanian armed forces would be under the command of the UAR. This was ominous enough but equally ominous was the fact that the King brought Ahmad Shuqayri, head of the so-called Palestine Liberation Organization and until recently at daggers drawn with the King, back to Amman with him for a triumphal reception. That Husayn felt impelled to take these two actions can be ascribed both to the internal unrest that had beset his country ever since the Samu' raid and to the deterioration of his relations with his Arab brothers. Right up to the outbreak of hostilities the experts were debating whether the King had been motivated more by internal or by inter-Arab considerations.

In Israel, there now began a period of preparedness that no one who lived through these hectic days is likely to forget. The call-up was greatly intensified and was extended to vehicles as well as men. Traffic diminished as cars were requisitioned and drivers left to join their units in the south. *Kol Israel* (the Voice of Israel) carried programs of greetings from soldiers in the field to their families. School children undertook the delivery of mail and the filling of sandbags and digging of trenches. Adults volunteered to do the work of men called to the colors and foreign volunteers began to arrive, 7,000 from the United States alone. People gave blood and civilian patients were evacuated from Hadassah and the other hospitals to the greatest extent possible. There were civil defense exercises and air raid drills. The Israeli authorities sent an engineer to the Consulate to advise us how best to take shelter in the event of bombing and what other precautions to take. Sandbags appeared in the entrances of many buildings in the New City.

There were some instances of panic in Israeli supermarkets but on the whole the public behaved very well. A sense of calm determination seemed to grip the people and petty quarrels were put aside. Morale was high, even though it was generally thought that in the event of war there would be severe air raids on the cities and heavy civilian casualties. The general attitude seemed to be that if the Arabs wanted a war they could have it, and the Israelis' greatest strength was that they knew what they were fighting for. As one observer has pointed out, for the Arabs, defeat would mean the loss of an army, for Israel it would mean the loss of everything. Everyone knew in his heart of hearts that if the Arabs came there would be a real bloodletting. As one officer said: "This would have been a second Masada, I'd have killed my wife and daughter to keep them out of the hands of the Arabs and I don't know anyone who didn't feel the same way."[3] For Israelis, this was truly their finest hour.

The situation in the Old City was in complete contrast. Virtually no precautions were taken by the authorities and the general atmos-

3 Churchill, p. 67.

phere was one of confidence. People talked constantly of impending war but seemed wholly unable to relate this to themselves personally. One Christian Arab doctor of our acquaintance who proposed setting up first aid stations was warned officially that any such move would immediately be taken by the Muslim majority as a sign of Christian conniving with the Jews and as evidence of foreknowledge of plotting by Israel to attack Jordan. It was not until after war had actually started that any Jordanian hospitals were commandeered by the Army, or civilian patients evacuated. This failure on the part of the Jordanians to take any precautions was evidence both of the generally more relaxed Arab attitude toward life, as compared with that in Israel, and of Arab overconfidence.

There was little panic buying in the Jordanian sector. After King Husayn's May 30 journey to Cairo, the Governor of the city, Anwar Khatib, called a meeting to organize civil defense but there was considerable opposition to the idea of distributing arms to the populace. One of those present is reported to have said "if we give the people arms they will use them against us." Anyone who spoke of popular resistance was apt to be regarded as a traitor who expected the Israelis to overrun the West Bank. It was not until the morning of June 5 that small quantities of arms were distributed to certain selected persons. Just before the war, a call came over the radio for volunteers to offer blood. A resident of the Old City who responded to this call and went to the local headquarters of the Red Crescent (equivalent of the Red Cross, in Muslim countries) was greeted by the staff with incredulity.[4] This, incidentally, was a great contrast to the situation in the Israeli sector, where Mayor Teddy Kollek told an American correspondent on May 29 that the authorities had had to stop collecting blood because there were no more facilities for storing it.

In these final days of May, one of my colleagues reported two rather ominous conversations which he had had with Jordanian contacts in the Old City. Both had made the most categorical threats as to what the Arabs would do to the New City if hostilities were to break out. They had pointed out that the Jordanian Arab Army had the New City under observation, from the heights to the north, east and south. They had warned that if the Israelis were to start something, their city would be blasted out of existence by Jordanian artillery. This was disconcerting, to say the least, to those of us who were residents of the New City, but it was just another illustration of Arab overconfidence. It was at this time that the Consular Corps

---

[4] Schleifer.

met and tried, unsuccessfully, to have Jerusalem declared an open city. Also at this juncture UNTSO decided to suspend the biweekly convoy to Mount Scopus, in view of the high degree of tension prevailing and the fear that the sight of the convoy might spark an attack by some foolhardy Arab, as had happened some years ago, with much loss of life.

In Israel, Foreign Minister Eban had returned from his trip abroad with nothing more from the Great Powers than the advice that Israel should not do anything rash but should stay its hand while the maritime nations tried to work out an international guarantee for the Strait of Tiran. As the situation grew more critical, there was a reorganization of the Israeli Cabinet and Moshe Dayan, regarded as an activist, became Minister of Defense, (he is reported to have commented: "It took 80,000 Egyptian soldiers to get me into the Cabinet.").[5] A new song, "Jerusalem the Golden," just composed and bearing prophetic overtones of the unification of the city, swept the country. As Laqueur points out, it was to become the "Tipperary" or the "Lili Marlene" of the Six Day War.[6] On the Arab side the singer Umm Kulthum popularized a song which ran: "We are going back by force of arms . . . Army of Arabism . . . the tragedy of Palestine pushes you toward the borders. All are with you in the flaming battle."[7] For its part, Damascus radio, echoing a speech by Nasir in which he declared "we are burning with desire" for war, proclaimed that the "whole nation" was ready to "wade through seas of blood."

By this time, we had sent out a second notice urging American citizens to leave, and most tourists had done so. Many of our resident citizens on both sides of the line elected to stay and only six out of nearly 500 American students at the Hebrew University left. Many foreign newspapermen were arriving in both Israel and Jordan—an indication that a real crisis was imminent.

While there was more of an air of crisis on the Israeli side, there were some signs just before the war broke out that Jordanians were getting anxious, too. On the last Friday before the war my wife took some time off from her temporary job in our consular section and went over to the Old City, with the idea of trying to reassure some of our Arab friends and acquaintances and to show them that we were not holed up with the Israelis for the duration. It was evident that the atmosphere in the Old City was changing. In the bazaar, she sensed the presence

[5] Churchill, p. 60.
[6] Laqueur, p. 154.
[7] Donovan, p. 90.

of fear in people's faces. They were waiting and watching for something; their voices were low and their steps cautious. At the butcher's, she stopped to buy two little legs of lamb (unavailable in the New City) and to exchange a friendly word. Down the street where the antiquarians, jewelers and rug merchants had their shops, all the gay and tantalizing objects, all the best temptations of the *suq*, were gone. In their places were cheap and tawdry pieces. Some of the metal shutters were already down, but some merchants were sitting there, silently awaiting the unexpected buyer. No, Talib told her, he had none of those embroidered dresses from Ramallah today. With a spreading of the hands and a shrug of the shoulders he indicated that after a time he would have something for our daughter. Meanwhile, would she please sit down for coffee.

It was unbearably hot: the air, like the footsteps and the voices, was utterly still; they talked quietly, but eventually frankness and fear came out into the open with hopeless, gesticulating questions: how had Nasir been able to trick and dupe the King and the leaders of the country? "How can we fight? We have nothing." After a while Talib looked at his watch and told her she should go home. Shuqayri was to harangue the crowds at noon, after prayers at the Dome of the Rock and no one could say what would happen then.

So Leila returned, stopping to speak to another merchant on the way. His eyes, too, were heavy-lidded and sad; a silent fear brooded in his shop. Back at our Old City apartment, she met with a friend who told her of families split with dissension, with some still thinking Nasir was the hope of the world and others regarding him as a veritable Mephistopheles. Fear. Anger with Amman, where "things had gone too far." Unpreparedness.

While my wife and I were lunching soon afterwards in the New City, we received word that 5,000 persons were marching from the Dome of the Rock to attack our Old City Consulate. We waited, full of apprehension, until finally word came that the mob had not numbered more than 2,000 and that the authorities had managed to divert it away from our premises. But it had been an anxious moment.

That weekend, Israelis flocked to the beaches: some said later this was a deliberate attempt by Dayan to lure the Arabs into a false state of security. In Amman, General Abd al-Munim Riyadh arrived from Cairo ready to assume charge of the Jordanian front, and on June 3 King Husayn, with prophetic accuracy, said at a press conference that there would be war within 48 hours.[8] On June 4 Iraq signed a defense

[8] Husayn, p. 55.

pact with the UAR and soon Iraqi troops began to arrive in Jordan—
President Arif had seen them off with the words "we shall meet in Tel
Aviv and Haifa."[9] King Husayn finally put Arab differences aside and
appealed to Syria for help. The order of the day issued June 3 by the
Egyptian Commander in Chief to the troops in the Sinai spoke of "the
Holy War through which you will . . . reconquer the plundered soil
of Palestine."[10]

It is now known that it was on Sunday, June 4, that the Israeli
Cabinet took the fateful decision to move first, before the Arabs. It
seems clear indeed that this was the only thing the Israelis could do.
The geography of the country meant that Israel had to take matters
into its own hands, once it concluded that war was inevitable. This
was essential if the Israelis were to forestall the two eventualities that
worried them the most: the pinching-off of the Jerusalem corridor and
the cutting of the country in two at its narrow waist, and massive air
raids on Israeli cities. It would appear that it was at this juncture that
the government determined that Israel's security was not going to be
assured by an international guarantee of the Strait, even if that were
forthcoming. In retrospect it seems equally clear that it was the Arab
leaders who were responsible for starting the June War. They had
duped themselves with their own fiery rhetoric, and had become
prisoners of their own propaganda. They thought they could win.

That same day, June 4, there were three separate shooting incidents
in Jerusalem that were referred to the Mixed Armistice Commission.
All three, it turned out, involved shooting by trigger-happy Jordanians,
an ominous prelude to the next day's events.

The Israeli air strike against Egyptian air bases and the advance into
Sinai took place early the next morning and the war was on. In Jerusalem, there was an alert about 8:00 a.m. and then an uneasy calm
prevailed until soon after 11:00 (someone said it was just 11:22)
when as I was sitting at my desk I heard firing break out all around.
The crack of rifles and machine guns and the crump of mortars as well
as heavier explosions from shells were to be with us for over 48 hours.
We often had the impression that the firing was going on only a few
yards away but our Marine Guards, on whom I depended for technical
information, assured me this was not the case. It was evident to us that,
in Jerusalem at least, the first shots were fired from the Arab side, and
indeed King Husayn concedes this in his book on the war.[11]

⁹ Laqueur, p. 100.
¹⁰ Churchill, p. 77.
¹¹ Husayn, p. 61.

Mandelbaum Gate closed immediately, cutting off all movement between the two sectors of the city. Seven of our Americans who were at the Old City Office at the time, with five of our local staff, endured for the next two days an ordeal which included constant fighting in the immediate vicinity, some thirteen direct hits which exploded inside the building, and the cutting of electric power, water and telephone. By a miracle, no one was hurt.[12]

In the New City we fared better, though we sustained one direct hit with shrapnel coming through several windows, including those of an office I had just vacated. On the third floor, where the offices were located, I established a command post type of operation and did not leave the building for days. Throughout, we remained in contact with our Old City office by our two-way radio and with Tel Aviv by telephone, and with Amman and Washington by telegraph.

With Marine guards, communications personnel, officers and employees, some UN personnel, and even two scared little girls off the street, we housed about thirty persons. Ten beds were made up in our living room for use in rotation. Meals were served in relays. In our annex across the garden we fed about twenty more, members of the staff and a few frightened American citizens who had taken refuge with us. Fortunately my wife and Carol Regan, a bride on her first Foreign Service assignment, had remained and could handle the logistics, which were complicated because we naturally had no idea how long our supplies were going to have to last. At the height of the fighting the Department ordered the evacuation of our remaining three wives (these two and Mrs. Hall, my deputy's wife, in the Old City) but as I informed my superiors with some asperity they were all working for me full time and in any event it would have been impossible to send them out with the heavy firing that was going on all around.

Most of the damage to buildings in the New City (some 1,300 private houses damaged in one way or another, plus a few direct hits on such institutions as the Israel Museum, Hadassah and other hospitals) was done in the first few hours that Monday, when the Jordanians distinctly had the upper hand. Then the Israelis moved in reinforcements and started to silence the Jordanian batteries. One of the earliest Jordanian direct hits had taken out the dome of the Dormition Abbey on Mount Zion, which the Israelis had been using as a military strongpoint since 1948. The greatest damage in the New

---

[12] See a moving account by Priscilla Hall, wife of my deputy, entitled "48 Hours in Jerusalem" in *Department of State Newsletter*, no. 76, August 1967.

City was in the Mea Shearim and Morasha (Musrara) quarters, adjoining no-man's land. The residents of the New City spent the entire period of hostilities in their shelters, which accounts for the low figure of only 15 civilians killed (of whom 11 were air-raid wardens). Considering the exposed nature of the Israeli sector, surrounded on three sides by Jordanian territory, it is remarkable that there was not more damage. The sturdy construction of the buildings was an important reason for this.

After the UN failed on the first morning to get agreement on a cease-fire, it became evident that we were in for some real fighting in the Jerusalem area. This was in complete contrast to the situation obtaining in 1956. Indeed, the authorities on both sides had made no effort to evacuate the civilian population and had even sent the children to school that morning. It was the rash decision of the UAR command in Jordan to use the Jordanian sector of Jerusalem as a base from which to attack the Israeli sector that led to the city's being involved in the war. It should have been apparent, given the characteristic tenacity of the Israelis in defending whatever territory they hold, that there would be a swift response to this provocation, as indeed there was, with far-reaching consequences. During the morning of June 5, King Husayn received a message from Israeli Prime Minister Eshkol, through the UN, saying Israel would not move if Jordan did not. The King tells us in his book, however, that it was too late when he received this message. The Israelis had already launched their assault in the south, and the Jordanians had started to bombard Jerusalem.[13] It is interesting to speculate what would have been the result if the Jordanians had received the Israelis' message sooner and if they had acted on it instead of being led (by the Egyptians) to commit the gross miscalculation which cost them so dearly.

The surprise attack on the city, with its indiscriminate shelling, gave the Israelis some real problems in the first few hours of the fighting. The great bulk of their troops were in the south and the Jerusalem area was held by a single brigade (known as the Jerusalem brigade) formed of reservists, who were to see some very heavy fighting in the next few days. As soon as it became evident that the Jordanians had launched a major attack against the city, the Israeli command ordered up a paratroop brigade (which was about to be flown to Sinai) and a mechanized brigade (which was guarding the coastal plain). These three units were given the task of counterattacking, to eliminate the positions from which the New City was being shelled, and to encircle

---

[13] Husayn, p. 64.

and take the Old City. The Israeli counterattack was greatly assisted by the fact that by this time the Jordanian air force had been wiped out. During the entire war we never saw a Jordanian plane over Jerusalem.

The Israeli air strikes against Egyptian, Jordanian and Syrian air bases were carried out with consummate skill and precision. A feature of the operation which contributed considerably to its success was the fact that the Israelis had in their armed forces Jews from all the various Arab countries, who could speak to the Arab pilots in their own particular dialect and who got on the air immediately, sowing confusion by broadcasting contradictory orders and instructions. In fact it was said after the war that during the entire period (admittedly a short one) that Arab pilots were in the air not one of them received any genuine instructions from his home base, so complete was the Israeli deception. The Israelis had done their homework thoroughly and knew the details of each target; some of their pilots had been practicing for years with models, for just this occasion. The Arabs, for their part, were disorganized and confused and their leaders did not trust each other.

The Israeli plan for the capture of the Old City as developed on June 5 was for the mechanized brigade to attack the heavily fortified Jordanian positions west and north of the city, cut the Jerusalem-Nablus highway, and swing south toward the city. Meanwhile the paratroop brigade would fight its way through the northern suburbs of the Old City and the Jerusalem brigade, which had captured Government House on the afternoon of June 5, would advance in an easterly direction, south of the Walled City and eventually link up with the other two forces. In their planning and execution the Israelis showed great imagination and flexibility whereas the Jordanians relied on a traditional, static defense with fixed positions heavily reinforced. The Israelis also undertook what is generally thought to be the most difficult assignment an army can have—of fighting in a built-up area such as this, with the added concern of trying to avoid damage to the Holy Places.[14]

Outside the Jerusalem area, there was some fighting that first day on the West Bank, north and south of the city, characterized by confusion and countermandering of orders on the Arab side and by complete mastery of the air on the Israeli side.

On the evening of that day, Monday, General Bull and several senior members of UNTSO came to our New City Consulate soon

---

[14] Kollek and Pearlman, p. 261; Churchill, p. 123 ff.

after their ejection from Government House (see Chapter V). The General asked if he could use one of our rooms for a staff meeting. As our living room was by then the men's dormitory, we let him use our bedroom, which thus became UN headquarters for a time. There he prepared his report to Secretary General U Thant of the day's fast moving events and then joined us for a quick meal.

After General Bull and his people left us, we prepared for an uneasy night. Heavy firing continued in the city and large fires could be seen burning in the vicinity of Government House. For the first time, in the late afternoon and evening we had become conscious of considerable Israeli air activity overhead, as the Israeli air force, its mission of destroying Arab air power accomplished, arrived to participate in the forthcoming battle for Jerusalem. Flares and searchlights lit up the city. At 2:30 a.m. Tuesday, very heavy firing broke out. This was the start of the paratroop attack through the northern suburbs, in the area just north of Mandelbaum Gate and in the vicinity of UNRWA headquarters, which were badly hit. According to all accounts, there occurred in this action the heaviest fighting for the city. The Israelis had to advance through five barbed wire fences and a large number of strongpoints which were stoutly defended by the Jordanians with great determination and courage. Around 6 a.m., the Israelis reached the American Colony, then continued on to take the Palestine Museum not long after. Some damage was done to the buildings of the American Colony but the indomitable Mrs. Bertha Vester remained holed up in her quarters throughout.

At about 5:30 that Tuesday morning I was called to our intercom to be told by my deputy in the Old City, Consul Pierson M. Hall, that our building there was under heavy and direct shellfire. I got in touch at once with the UN and with our two Embassies in Amman and Tel Aviv in an effort to get both sides to spare our building but I doubt whether I accomplished much. I should explain here that our building was caught in the crossfire in the bitter fighting that was raging outside, especially in and around the Old City YMCA next door where the Jordanian Army had forcibly established a position on the roof. It is impossible to say which side was responsible for the damage and there is no reason to suppose that either side deliberately fired at our building. At no time, incidentally, did it shelter any Jordanian snipers although this was alleged afterwards by some Israelis and most regrettably picked up by *Newsweek*.

During the day the mechanized brigade which had been sent around west and north of the Old City joined up with the paratroopers who had fought their way through the northern suburbs in the heavy hand-to-hand combat just described. These units began to consolidate their position in the area outside the inner city, in the face of fierce Arab resistance. There was some sniping from houses at the Israeli troops and some Jordanian soldiers put on civilian dress and continued to fight on. The Israeli radio warned the inhabitants of the Old City to stay indoors and to put out white flags as a sign of surrender.

In Amman, meanwhile, King Husayn realized, as early as the morning of June 6, that the situation of his forces in Jerusalem and on the West Bank was rapidly becoming hopeless. He telephoned President Nasir to say Jordan either would have to accept an immediate cease-fire or withdraw from the West Bank. Nasir, however, was unwilling at this stage to agree. This conversation between the two leaders is the one that was monitored by the Israelis and broadcast over the Israeli radio—we heard it shortly afterwards. It contained the allegation by Nasir and Husayn, wholly without foundation and later denied by both, that British and American planes were fighting with the Israelis. By mid-day, Husayn was losing tanks at the rate of one every ten minutes and was expecting the Israelis to arrive in Amman any time. He sent another urgent message to Cairo. Finally, at 11:15 p.m., revealing for the first time that he had lost his air force and conceding that the Arabs had been defeated, Nasir agreed to the evacuation of the West Bank. This, however, was too late to prevent the complete rout of the Jordanian Army and the loss (mainly as a result of Israeli air action) of nearly all its heavy equipment, in fighting in the north as well as in the Jerusalem area.[15]

By the evening of Tuesday, June 6, the Israelis virtually had the Walled City of Jerusalem surrounded. Its actual capture was their next objective but first they would have to complete their occupation of the two hills of Mount Scopus and the Mount of Olives, with the Augusta Victoria Hospital on the saddle between them, since these hills dominated the eastern approach to the Walled City. They first planned to carry out this clearing operation on the evening of the sixth but upon receiving a report (never confirmed) that the Jordanians were bringing up tanks from the Jericho area decided to wait until Wednesday morning.

Back in the New City Consulate, we had managed during the day to get rid of some of our uninvited guests (particularly after the explosion in quick succession that morning of five Arab shells that sent shrapnel through our garden and windows, one of which scored a

[15] Husayn, p. 80 ff.

direct hit on our annex building). My next door neighbor, who took rather a lurid view of Arab intentions, and whose own windows were shattered by the blast, was convinced that this was the act of some desperate Jordanian gunner, zeroing in on the Consulate from some position in the Old City from which our flag was visible, but I doubt it. That same evening I spoke to Hall on the intercom and asked how things were going in the Old City office. He replied fine, they were just sitting down to a candlelight supper (naturally, as they had no electricity) and were trying to decide whether to have red wine or white. It was Hall who, earlier that day, while heavy firing was still going on all around the Old City building, had taken an American flag as protection and gone out into the streets to check on the safety of American citizens and to make sure our official vehicles were safe— an act which later earned him the Department's Superior Service Award.

Wednesday morning, the final assault on the Walled City began. First came the aerial bombardment of the Augusta Victoria Hospital with rockets and napalm, which I watched from our New City roof. The hospital was suspected, incorrectly, by the Israelis to be harboring Jordanian troops. The Israelis then completed their occupation of the Mount of Olives and, after a ten-minute artillery bombardment of the Muslim quarter, the extreme northeast section of the Walled City, stormed through St. Stephen's Gate and into the Walled City itself. It was just before 10:00 o'clock. As the first troops reached the Haram al-Sharif (the Temple Mount to the Jews) the Governor and other Arab dignitaries appeared and surrendered the city. There was virtually no fighting in the Walled City and the Israeli forces had orders to use no heavy weapons and to spare the Holy Places (most of which emerged unscathed). Within a few minutes, the Israelis were at the Wailing Wall. Shortly thereafter, the Chief Chaplain of the armed forces arrived to lead prayers and sound the *shofar,* or ram's horn, which is reserved for only the most solemn of occasions in Judaism. Men wept with joy as they kissed the stones of the Wall, and the leaders of Israel came to pay their homage. Moshe Dayan asserted: "We have returned to the holiest of our Holy Places, never to be parted from it again."

At mid-day I again went up to the roof of our New City building to see the Israeli soldiers who had raised their flag on the city wall and were mounting guard over the walls from the same positions the Jordanians had occupied for 19 years. This virtually marked the end of the fighting in the Jerusalem area. By evening of that day the Israelis had completed their occupation of the entire West Bank. In the New

City we stayed on an emergency basis for a couple of days more and then disbanded our mess and dormitory.

To round out this brief summary of the June War, I might recall that as soon as fighting broke out June 5 the Security Council of the United Nations met in New York to consider the situation. A resolution providing for a cease-fire was endlessly debated that day and the next, with the Soviet representative insisting that Israel must withdraw from the territory it had seized. Late on Wednesday, a cease-fire was accepted by Jordan and Israel, and the following day, by the UAR and Israel; the Jordanian cease-fire, however, was not effective on the whole front until the 8th. On June 9, 10 and 11 took place the lightning campaign in which the Israelis took from the Syrians the hills, called by the Israelis the Golan Heights, from which the Syrians had attacked Israeli settlements in the upper Jordan Valley for so many years. When agreement for a cease-fire on the front was reached late on the 11th the war was over.

The Jordanians were generally credited by the Israelis and others with having put up the best fight on the Arab side. It is interesting to note that in spite of Syrian bellicosity the Syrians did practically nothing in the first few days of the war, and that when the Israelis overran their fortified positions on the Golan Heights they were found to be completely dug in, with no capability of taking offensive action. The Syrians were housed in elaborate bunkers and even had their families staying with them. They had apparently made no preparations for an advance. The Syrians also failed the Jordanians badly, following King Husayn's appeal for help. It was not until 8:20 p.m. on June 7, when the war was already over for the Hashimite Kingdom, that the first Syrian troops arrived at the frontier, only to turn around and return home at once to join in the fighting on the Syrian front. The Egyptian rout is too familiar to need recounting here. The Iraqis sent a brigade which never got as far as the river Jordan and which was badly mauled from the air. The Lebanese did not participate in the war. And that summarizes the Arab war effort.

Randolph and Winston Churchill relate in their book on the war a revealing remark made to one of them just afterwards by General Ezer Weizmann, a top Israeli military leader, when he said:

> You must understand why Israel was built here rather than in Uganda or Canada. We could never have fought the way we have for a Jewish state in any other part of the world. Jerusalem, the West Bank of the Jordan, indeed the whole of Palestine has a very deep significance for us. It is the basis of Zionism.[16]

---

[16] Churchill, p. 147.

Right after the end of hostilities, conditions in the Old City were chaotic, with no electric power, water or telephone, with dead bodies in the streets and with most shops closed. White flags fluttered from the houses. Few buildings in the neighborhood of our Old City Consulate were completely destroyed but several, including ours, bore the scars of heavy shelling. Estimates of civilians killed were hard to come by but the most accurate seems to have been about 300 for the whole of the Jordanian sector. Most of these were within the Walled City, which sustained its most serious damage during the artillery bombardment of the Muslim quarter on the morning of June 7. This preceded the storming of the inner city by Israeli paratroopers and was intended to take out Jordanian military positions that were still holding out in that area. This was when the Crusader Church of St. Anne, the most seriously damaged of all the Holy Places, was hit—undoubtedly not intentionally. I had one of my officers make a survey of damage to the Holy Places and he reported that there had been relatively little except for St. Anne's. Again, as in the New City, it is remarkable that casualties or damage were not greater, considering the fierceness of the fighting that took place at some points.

The slopes of Mount Scopus and the Mount of Olives were littered with cases of ammunition, unused and hurriedly abandoned by the retreating Jordanian army. Great numbers of vehicles, including tanks, had been captured intact and were being driven off by the Israelis.

An interesting comparison of the state of organization of the two armies was related to us by Arab friends whose house lay directly in the path of the Israeli advance toward Mount Scopus and who thus saw a good deal of the fighting. On Tuesday morning, just before the Israelis captured this particular part of the city, a Jordanian tank nearby was hit and burst into flames. One of the crew managed to get out and ran to our friends' house, begged for food and water, saying he had had nothing to eat or drink for 48 hours. He was given something and told to leave at once, as the Israelis were obviously about to take over the area. For days after our friends could see the Israeli convoys passing by three times a day with rations, neatly packaged in plastic, one for each Israeli soldier.

Our most immediate problem was the state of our Old City Consulate. The Halls, whose apartment on the upper floor had been badly damaged, had already moved to the American School of Oriental Research, which I had taken over temporarily with the approval of the School's headquarters in the United States. Fortunately we were able through Israeli friends to arrange for repairs to our Consulate to begin almost immediately, and also to have unexploded shells removed from our garden.

Another problem we faced was that of getting around the Old City and the West Bank, as we had some 1,300 American citizens in the area to look after. Regulations and passes were changed with great frequency. Indeed the confusion among the occupation authorities was so total that it seemed clear to us that the Israelis, whatever military plans they may have had, did not have a plan for the administration of so large an area, with an Arab population of about one million. For some time these problems of movement throughout our district and of answering hundreds of inquiries about the safety of our citizens absorbed our energies to such an extent that I was moved to complain to the Department, using the words of Sherlock Holmes to Dr. Watson in the *Adventure of the Copper Beeches,* that our office "seems to be degenerating into an agency for recovering lost lead pencils and giving advice to young ladies from boarding schools."

We found from the very start that we were able to make use of our special position in Jerusalem to be of help. It was a unique experience, that first day that I crossed to the Old City after the war, to encounter at occupation headquarters both the Mayor of the Old City, Rawhi al-Khatib, and the Mayor of the New City, soon to be Mayor of all Jerusalem, Teddy Kollek, and to introduce them to each other, as they had never met before. This first contact between the two mayors was a fleeting one, as Mayor al-Khatib was still under detention. It was touching to have him ask me to tell his wife that he was alive and to see her face when I did so.

The Israelis at first stationed troops in Augusta Victoria Hospital, which made the functioning of the hospital very difficult (the lower floors were still usable in spite of the Israeli air attack which had gutted the top of the building). We passed the word to Israeli contacts and the soldiers were withdrawn the next day. In connection with the attack on the hospital it was gratifying to learn that shortly after hostilities a delegation from the *Knesset* called at the hospital to tender an official apology, that blood was immediately donated by New City hospitals and that the ruptured water supply was promptly reconnected. One of my doctor friends at Augusta Victoria, who had every reason to be bitter because all his papers, with the results of twenty years' research, had been destroyed in the air attack, remarked to me that he had been particularly touched by the offer of Jewish blood for Arab wounded. That the Israelis did this, he commented, showed that they really wanted to help.

Another instance where we were able to be of assistance was in connection with the residents of the area near the Wailing Wall whose houses were razed in the first few days of the occupation to make room for the thousands of Jewish pilgrims coming to visit the Wall. We learned that these people had been turned out on very short notice, sometimes a matter of minutes, and allowed to take with them only such things as they could carry, before their houses were bulldozed. Leila visited them and found that 129 families, nearly 1,000 persons in all, were destitute and homeless, some occupying an old *khan* or market, others in an unfinished school or any other spot they could find. Through the US-Israel surplus commodity program, we were able to arrange with Israeli friends for foodstuffs to be sent across to a convent in the Walled City where they were distributed in minimal quantity to the neediest. This tided them over until international relief agencies took charge.

The same razing and bulldozing near the Wailing Wall gave rise to a problem of a different sort. For some time extensive restoration work had been going on at the Church of the Holy Sepulchre. Large quantities of a special kind of stone from a quarry near Bethlehem had been brought to the Walled City and stored in an area which happened to be near the Wailing Wall. During the clearing operations, this stone was buried under several yards of rubble. While some work on the Church was continued, the fact that the Arab stonecutters involved were paid only when the stone was delivered to the Church (not to the place of storage) caused considerable hardship, coupled with the closing of all Old City banks and the resultant scarcity of cash for wages. Eventually, after we left Jerusalem, some of the stone was uncovered.

A feature of our daily life during this period was the constant sound of explosions as mines in the no-man's land were detonated and buildings razed to open up a number of access routes from the New to the Old City. Many of the buildings in question had been in ruins since the 1948 fighting and were certainly an eyesore. Thus the work constituted an improvement in the appearance of the city. Occasionally, however, the Israeli army engineers showed an excess of zeal and blew up the wrong building. We knew of two persons who lost their homes in this way. We also knew of several cases where windows that had been shattered during the war and replaced were again broken during the demolitions. Certainly more houses were destroyed through these operations than during the war.

We also continued to hear occasional shots, sometimes from snipers who we were told were still hiding out in the dark alleyways of the Walled City or from soldiers shooting at would-be looters trying to sneak across from the New City. Immediately after the war, we heard of an instance where some 80 Arab soldiers were found holed up in a convent in the Walled City, in civilian dress. Fortunately they gave themselves up, or the Israelis would surely have blown up the convent.

On the first Friday after the war that Muslims from the Israeli side were permitted to cross to pray at the Haram al-Sharif, one of my officers was a witness to something that might have turned out to be serious. Thousands of persons had congregated at the Noble Enclosure and the Israeli authorities apparently feared that some incident might take place. At all events, my colleague happened to be driving up the Mount of Olives in the direction of the Inter-Continental Hotel, which commands a superb view of the Haram al-Sharif. He was turned back by Israeli soldiers but not before he had had an opportunity to see four tanks with their guns trained on the Mosque enclosure. Whether they would have actually fired deliberately on Islam's third most Holy Place if there had been trouble will never be known, since no untoward incidents occurred, but the implications were disturbing.

When my wife and I had learned of the fall of the Old City to the Israeli forces, we said to each other with heavy hearts that none of our Old City friends would ever speak to us again (this was at the time when Arab opinion was being inflamed by the unfounded allegation that our planes had fought with the Israelis). When we got over to the Jordanian side, however, and started to look up our friends, we found them glad to see us and pathetically grateful for the packages of food that we took them (they had been without cooked food for days). By a miracle, everyone was safe but one had only to look at their faces to see what they had been through. Unlike our neighbors in the New City they had no shelters to go to but the thick walls of their houses had stood them in good stead. Our New City friends were all safe, too, but curiously enough we found them to be a bit prickly in their attitude and inclined to be critical when we told them that the war had brought hardship to the residents of the other side.

We were naturally interested in learning what had happened to our archaeologist friends and to the archaelogical institutions in the Old City. There was intense speculation as to the fate of the Dead Sea Scrolls, as it was known the Jordanians had had plans to take them to Amman. Of course the collection would be of the greatest interest to Israeli archaeologists, and we knew that the Israeli Director of

Antiquities, Dr. Avram Biran, had rushed over to the Old City while the firing was still going on, early on the morning of June 6, to take charge of the Palestine Musuem as soon as it was occupied by the paratroopers. When the Museum was formally reopened by the Israelis in mid-July the wing containing the Scrolls was sealed off and it remained so. Eventually we learned that the Scrolls had not been taken to Amman and were intact.

Soon after the war a local antique dealer who had for some years kept an original Dead Sea Scroll hidden away came to Leila with a bizarre tale. It was evident that the Israelis knew of the existence of this Scroll, for on coming to the Old City they immediately went to his home and seized the Scroll. They took him to Tel Aviv for several days' questioning, and then released him. He told us he had come into possession of the Scroll, which he claimed had a value of a million dollars, when some Bedouin from the Qumran area brought it to him. An American visitor to the Old City prior to the war, who had crossed through the Mandelbaum Gate with a tiny fragment of the Scroll that the dealer had given him in hopes he would buy it, had apparently revealed its existence to the Israeli Department of Antiquities. The dealer never got the Scroll back and eventually it was revealed to the world as the so-called Temple Scroll.

The fathers at the *Ecole Biblique,* not far from our Old City Consulate, had a difficult time during the fighting. At 8:00 a.m. Tuesday June 6, Israeli soldiers entered their compound, looking for snipers, of whom there were none, and ordered the fathers, some of whom were venerable men of world reputation like Père de Vaux, to line up against the wall, hands up, in three hour shifts, day and night. Their Jordanian employees were taken away and did not return for over three weeks. The Israelis installed a machine gun post in the tower of the Church, which in turn drew fire, apparently from Israeli artillery in error, but in any event causing considerable damage to the tower. The reason for the treatment accorded to the Dominican fathers at the *Ecole Biblique* seems to have been that on the morning of June 5 the Jordanians had set up two mortar positions in a vacant lot adjoining the School, and had fired from these positions into the New City. To Israeli spotters half a mile away it could have looked as though mortar shells were coming from the *Ecole Biblique* itself. This is confirmed by the discovery by an American archaeologist in a house near no-man's land known to have been occupied by Israeli paratroopers just before their assault on the night of June 5-6, of a map of the city with a circle drawn around the School.

Down the street from the *Ecole Biblique* stands a girls' school where there occurred an instance of chivalry between the opposing forces. Two Jordanian soldiers took refuge on the roof of the school and began firing on the advancing Israeli troops. When the latter reached the school they demanded that the two Jordanians come down and surrender. They sent a message to this effect up to the roof once, twice, three times. Each time the reply came back that the two men would never surrender but would fight to the death. Finally, the Israelis turned their backs for a few minutes and gave these brave men a chance to slip away, which they did.

An immediate problem that developed in the Old City was that of looting. The crack troops who took the city, such as the parachutists, behaved correctly but soon they were all replaced by less disciplined reservists. There was no rape and little personal violence but looting by soldiers and civilians was widespread. Cars, hotel and house furnishings and all luxury goods, prohibitively priced under Israel's austerity economy, were regarded as fair prize of war. In the first few days we saw truckloads of goods of all kinds going through the Mandelbaum Gate on their way into the Israeli sector. The military authorities eventually began to cope with this problem but it was hard to control, even with the stiff legal penalties that were threatened.

Most instances of looting were not so blatant as that experienced by a well-known antique dealer in the Walled City whom we knew well. His shop was entered during the curfew hours by Israeli uniformed military, including an officer, and stripped of many priceless icons and other works of art. Some of these were recovered after vigorous protests were lodged with the military authorities by New City archaeologists who came to this man's defense. Many of our acquaintances, however, lost possessions, especially automobiles. For a while most of our Old City friends went about on foot but gradually cars started to come back, as the military authorities began to crack down. Hotels, grocery stores which stocked imported items, and dealers in electrical appliances unavailable in Israel also suffered heavy losses. This looting continued until there was little left. Meanwhile, many claims for compensation were brought to our attention but there was little that we could do since the owners were rarely American citizens. One minor but irritating aspect of the stealing was that we had to station a guard outside our Old City building to prevent the American flags from being lifted off our parked cars.

During this period there continued the movement of persons from the West Bank to the East Bank of the Jordan that had started during the war and that has now (1969) involved some 400,000 persons, of whom about half are described as "old" and about half as "new" refugees. Those who left during and immediately after the war were mostly people from the refugee camps in the Jericho area who panicked, or people who did not want to become separated from their families on the East Bank or people who simply did not want to live under the Israelis. For some time the Israeli authorities provided free bus service from the Old City to the Jordan River for those desiring to leave, provided they signed a paper saying they were going of their own free will. The refusal of the authorities to allow more than a handful (14,000) to return has been a sore point.

While we had no evidence at this time that the Israelis were following a deliberate policy of forcing these people out, there were instances of their destroying certain border villages, that is, villages lying along the former Armistice lines, and moving out the inhabitants. These were places where the Israelis had reason to believe, or sometimes merely suspected, that sabotage raids or artillery bombardments had been mounted against Israeli settlements. The fact that the Israelis had for years seen their own border villages exposed to irresponsible and outrageous attack had of course been a contributing factor to the outbreak of war. The Arab villages in question were also places which had offered a strategic or topographical advantage and would do so again if the former borders were restored. A typical instance was Qalqiliya[17] to the northwest of Jerusalem, across from the narrow waist of Israel where the country was less than ten miles wide.

As related to me by the Mayor of Qalqiliya, the Israelis came into the town on June 6 after a brief battle in which little damage was done. They then put the Mayor in a jeep equipped with a loudspeaker and handed him a paper already prepared in Arabic which he was asked to read out and which was an appeal to the inhabitants to leave at once, on the grounds that the town was about to be bombed by Iraqi planes. This caused considerable panic and almost everyone left in the direction of Nablus. After the town had been evacuated, Israeli soldiers systematically dynamited a large number of houses, estimated at some 75 per cent of the dwellings. The alleged reason was that the town had harbored snipers and had been used as base from which artillery had fired on Tel Aviv (only about 12 miles distant).

The villagers, camping out on the charity of the people of Nablus, naturally wanted to go home. Permission was refused for some time but eventually, after the Mayor had intervened with Moshe Dayan and

---

[17] United Nations, *Gussing Report*, p. 14 ff.

with UNRWA, authorization was given for them to return. The Israelis also promised to help rebuild the village but when I visited Qalqiliya shortly before my departure nothing had been done.

One footnote to the story of Qalqiliya: there never was an Iraqi air raid on the town, nor did more than one or two shells fall on Tel Aviv during the entire war, though a few fell on Tel Aviv's airport at Lydda nearby.

Other instances of destruction were at Imwas (thought by some to be the Biblical Emmaus) and Bayt Nuba and Yalu near Latrun and at Bayt Awwa west of Hebron.[18] French priests in the neighborhood told us of the fate of Imwas. There was considerable fighting in the area and for several days the inhabitants of the three villages sheltered in the monastery at Latrun. After the shooting was over, the Israelis came to the monastery and told the villagers they could return home. The people from Imwas were escorted to the village by the soldiers and as soon as they arrived were asked to stand to one side. The village was then demolished, house by house, and the rubble bulldozed (later reports say trees have been planted on the site). The villagers fled in panic to the neighborhood of Ramallah, along with the residents of Bayt Nuba and Yalu which had suffered the same fate.

It was said that the reason for the harsh treatment of the people of Imwas was that on the night of June 4-5, just before hostilities broke out, a group of UAR commandos who had been sent across the river Jordan from Amman arrived in the Imwas area, unknown to the villagers, and were infiltrated into Israeli territory on a sabotage mission. They were all caught by the Israelis and on interrogation said they came from Imwas, hence, the punishment of the whole village. No reason was given for the demolition of the other two villages nearby or of Bayt Awwa further south. Only in the case of the last named (and of Qalqiliya) were the inhabitants permitted to return.

The Israeli authorities were evidently anxious not to have anything known about these incidents. The road to Imwas and the two neighboring villages was closed and no one allowed to pass—I myself was refused permission. An American newspaperman to whom I happened to mention the story decided to try to run it down. For several days he was given the run around by the Israeli military but finally after much persuasion was taken to Imwas under the escort of an Israeli colonel who said that the destruction had taken place during the very heavy fighting that had raged all around the village. By chance they

---

[18] *Gussing Report*, p. 16 *ff.*; see also *Report of Deputation of National Council of Churches, July 19-31, 1968.*

encountered one of the priests who to the colonel's embarrassment related the version of the incident as given above.

On June 28, following the passage of special legislation by the *Knesset* the preceding day, the Old City was brought under Israeli municipal administration. The way in which this was done was interesting. The *Knesset* passed a law authorizing the government to extend its administration to any part of "Eretz Israel" that it might see fit. The term "Eretz Israel," which is a Biblical, almost mystical, term meaning Land of Israel, is not customarily used in current Israeli legislation. "Eretz Israel" was used by Jews over the centuries to refer to the land whence their ancestors came, the Land of the Bible, and was the term which the Jewish Community in Mandate days used in referring to Palestine. It is not, however, necessarily limited to the area of the Palestine Mandate. It could conceivably be applied not only to the Old City or the West Bank but to other areas where the Jews lived in antiquity, including areas east of the Jordan.

At all events, the Israeli Minister of the Interior issued a decree under this law extending Israeli municipal jurisdiction to the whole of the city of Jerusalem as newly defined. The boundaries of the city on the Arab side were greatly extended, to take in not only the Walled City and the territory nearby which had been under the Jordanian municipality, but the modern quarter developed since 1948, Mount Scopus, the Mount of Olives, and the whole area extending as far north as Kalandia Airport (see map 4).

While government spokesmen denied that this action constituted annexation, it was hard to see where the distinction lay, particularly as a sharp line began to be drawn between "East Jerusalem," which was no longer regarded as being under military occupation, and the occupied West Bank. Residents of the West Bank had to obtain permits to enter the city limits, as newly defined, and customs checkpoints were set up on the roads. On the other hand, any resident of Jerusalem, including an Arab resident, was free to travel anywhere in Israel.

As soon as the city was opened up to free passage back and forth (the Mandelbaum Gate checkpoint was abolished) Arabs and Jews began thronging in either direction across the former barriers. This was an extraordinary experience for anyone who had known pre-war Jerusalem. We had the unique experience of receiving Israeli friends in the Old City and Jordanian friends in the New City. While this mingling of the two populations went well on the whole, and while there were many instances of old acquaintances meeting again, it would be too much to say that all scars had healed. The relations between the two halves of the population remained uneasy.

After the opening up of the city we started in a quiet way to bring Israeli and Jordanian friends together in our house: doctors who had heard of each other's work but who had never met, women engaged in social welfare activities on either side, or lawyers who had worked in the same office in the days of the Mandate. We called this "Operation Handclasp," and hoped in this way to help break down barriers, although we had to move cautiously as people's susceptibilities were easily aroused.

To this period belongs the story of the piano. Ever since the 1948 war there had been in the living room of the Consulate General in the New City a very fine Bechstein grand which had been left with the then Consul General for safekeeping by an Arab who had fled to the Old City. Periodically the owner would come to our Old City office and ask if he could have his piano back. He was always told there was no way of getting it through the Mandelbaum Gate but if he could arrange to have it shipped via Haifa to Athens, say, and transshipped to Beirut and on to the Old City by truck, he was free to do so. Shortly after the opening up of the city he happily claimed his piano.

Almost at once, the occupation gave rise to a number of problems, in the religious and economic fields particularly.[19] Soon after the war the then Prime Minister Levi Eshkol held a meeting with all religious leaders and gave assurances that Israel intended to guarantee access to all the Holy Places and to respect the sites. He also proposed that the actual maintenance of the sites should be in the hands of the religious sects themselves. Unfortunately not all of them acted upon this offer and problems continued to arise.

First of all, the Muslims and Christians objected to the fact that formal control of all the Holy Places were vested in the Israeli Ministry of Religious Affairs, which was dominated by Orthodox Jews. The Muslims made so vigorous a complaint that a change was made, but control of the Christian sites remained under this Ministry.

Friction also arose over the behavior of the thousands of Israelis who flocked to the Old City as soon as it was opened up to them. These sightseers, both civilian and military, swarmed into the mosques and churches. Hardly any of them had ever been in a church or mosque before. Their conduct, and the dress of the women, many in short shorts, was not always decorous. Guns, babies and dogs taken into

---

[19] United Nations, *Thalmann Report*, gives description of conditions in Old City as observed in August and September 1967.

churches or mosques gave rise to varying degrees of protest and some unseemly behavior raised cries of desecration. Since the religious authorities (often pusillanimous) dared to do little to correct matters it was left to the Israeli military to do so. Gradually some order and discipline were restored but the basic issue that Israel was in occupation of the sites remained.

In the economic field, the occupation brought a host of problems, as tourism, a vital source of income, fell off sharply and unemployment soared. The residents of the Old City were forced to convert their Jordanian dinars into Israeli pounds at a rate fixed arbitrarily low. Israeli income taxes were imposed and also customs duties, even when Jordanian duties had already been paid on the same merchandise. One of the local employees in our Old City Consulate, whose salary doubled when we had to put him on the Israeli wage scale, was the sole support of 21 members of his family. None of the others could find work. The bank system was disrupted by the fact that the Old City banks had all been branches of banks in Amman, to which deposits were transferred daily. Their accounts were frozen, and remain so to this day. Thus there was little cash available in the Old City. The cutting-off economically of the West Bank both from the East Bank and the Old City, in the initial stages of the occupation, also caused great hardship. Unemployment was increased by the dismissal of the Old City Municipal Council (including Mayor al-Khatib) and the dissolution of the Arab Municipality, although some of the more menial employees were kept on in their jobs. Some Arab laborers took jobs in the Israeli sector, in order to continue living, but people of the professional class were reluctant to do so.

Immediately after hostilities a number of our Palestinian friends on the West Bank and in the Old City had said to us that they were prepared to make their peace with the Jews. They had backed the wrong horse for 19 years and they wanted no more of Nasir and Husayn. As time went on, however, and the Israelis gave every sign of strengthening their hold on the Old City, our Arab friends grew disillusioned and restive. The reprisals taken against border villages, the looting, the religious and economic problems, the refusal to readmit those who had fled, all combined to cause doubts regarding Israeli intentions. Even before our departure, these various sources of dissatisfaction had given rise to boycotts and general strikes, and it was not long before more violent forms of resistance became manifest. I report these developments not simply to rehearse an old story but to try to place things in perspective and to suggest that not all was so rosy as

Map 1. Israel and Its Arab Neighbors

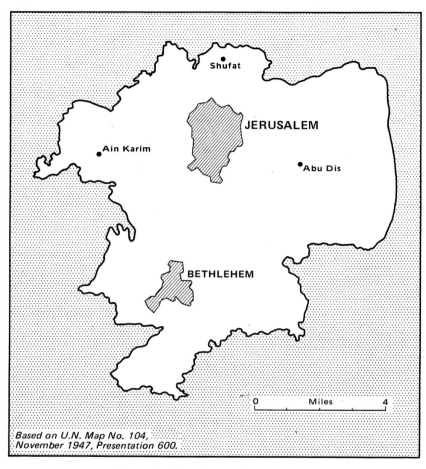

Map 2. The Corpus Separatum

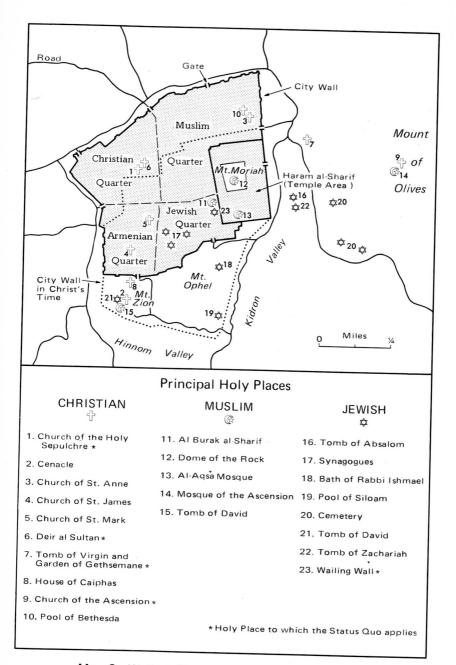

Principal Holy Places

CHRISTIAN ✝	MUSLIM ℭ	JEWISH ✡
1. Church of the Holy Sepulchre *	11. Al Burak al-Sharif	16. Tomb of Absalom
2. Cenacle	12. Dome of the Rock	17. Synagogues
3. Church of St. Anne	13. Al-Aqsa Mosque	18. Bath of Rabbi Ishmael
4. Church of St. James	14. Mosque of the Ascension	19. Pool of Siloam
5. Church of St. Mark	15. Tomb of David	20. Cemetery
6. Deir al Sultan *		21. Tomb of David
7. Tomb of Virgin and Garden of Gethsemane *		22. Tomb of Zachariah
8. House of Caiphas		23. Wailing Wall *
9. Church of the Ascension *		
10. Pool of Bethesda		

*Holy Place to which the Status Quo applies

Map 3. Walled City and Principal Holy Places

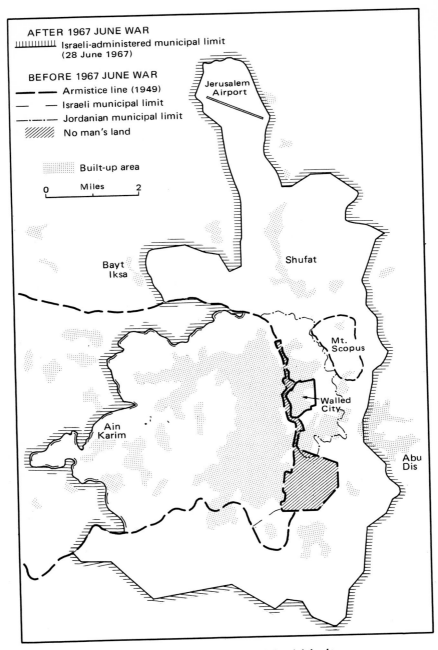

AFTER 1967 JUNE WAR

|||||||||| Israeli-administered municipal limit
(28 June 1967)

BEFORE 1967 JUNE WAR

━ ━ Armistice line (1949)

— — Israeli municipal limit

—.—.— Jordanian municipal limit

▨ No man's land

▨ Built-up area

0   Miles   2

Jerusalem
Airport

Bayt
Iksa

Shufat

Mt.
Scopus

Ain
Karim

Walled
City

Abu
Dis

Map 4. Jerusalem: Municipal Limits

Israeli reports have suggested, after the "clean surgical operation," as the Israelis in their postwar euphoria liked to call the war.

As the days drew on I reminded my Department that it had long been planned that I would be leaving Jerusalem during that summer, and an August 15 departure date was agreed upon. Our last days were filled with preparation for our departure and with farewells, particularly nostalgic for us, both because of our long association with the Holy City and because of the traumas that the war had brought. Finally, on the early morning of the 15th, we went for the last time down the familiar road to the airport and took one last look back at the city, on its hilltops, an unforgettable sight. It was the end of a chapter, and a unique one, in our lives, for as Sir Ronald Storrs so truly says, "there is no promotion after Jerusalem."[20]

Sources: A good deal of the material in this chapter is of course based on personal experience. I have also drawn on the press, both local and international, for the period prior to, during and subsequent to the June War. The literature on the war is voluminous. A selection of leading titles will be found in the Bibliography. The most useful straight accounts of the war itself I have found to be Churchill: *The Six Day War,* and Donovan (ed.): *Israel's Fight for Survival,* both of which appeared in paperback shortly after the end of the war. A recent, more detailed, work is Safran's *From War to War.*

Most sources tell the story from the Israeli side and it is therefore important to get the Arab point of view. The best such accounts are King Husayn's book *My "War" with Israel* and an article ("The Fall of Jerusalem") by Abdullah Schleifer, an American Muslim resident of the Old City, which appeared in the *Evergreen Review* for December 1967.

The battle for Jerusalem is described in Churchill, *op. cit.,* and Donovan, *op. cit.,* as well as Safran, *op. cit.,* and Kollek and Pearlman: *Jerusalem, A History of Forty Centuries.* See also a series of articles sent to the *Chicago Tribune* by its correspondent Arthur Veysey, who was in the city before, during and after the war (on both sides) and whose reporting covers the period May 25 - July 1. There are also the first-hand accounts of American archaeologists in Jerusalem, on both sides, in the *Newsletters* of the American Schools of Oriental Research, Nos. 1, 2, 4-5, 7 and 10, 1967-68; *The Biblical Archaeologist,* Vol. XXX, Nos. 3 and 4, September and December, 1967, and two newsletters of the Hebrew Union College–Jewish Institute of Religion, dated June 7 and 28, 1967.

The best account of the background of the war is an article in *Foreign Affairs* for January 1968, by Charles W. Yost, entitled "How the Arab-Israel War Began." See also John S. Badeau: *The American Approach to the Arab World,* and an article in the *Atlantic Monthly* for December 1967; Khouri, *The Arab-Israeli Dilemma;* and Laqueur, *The Road to Jerusalem* (especially the chapter on Israeli preparedness entitled "Konenut").

[20] The *Memoirs* of Sir Ronald Storrs, p. 465.

VII

The Problem of the Holy Places

The significance of the Holy Places as an issue in international politics arises from the fact, alluded to in Chapter II, that just as Palestine is the Holy Land of the world's three great monotheistic religions, so is Jerusalem their Holy City.[1] In that chapter I cited the Temple area (or Haram al-Sharif) as an illustration of the way in which the shrines sacred to all three are so intermingled as to make it impossible to separate them from each other. This is not the only example, however. Others are Mount Zion, the site of the Cenacle, or Room of the Last Supper (for which it is sacred to Christians), and of the Tomb of David, sacred to both Muslims and Jews, David being one of those Old Testament figures who is revered by all three religions. The Mount of Olives and Bethany, both of which have special associations with the life of Our Lord, happen also to be the sites of Muslim shrines. Jewish tombs are scattered over the slopes of the Mount of Olives and are in close proximity to the Garden of Gethsemane, as are Muslim graves near the city wall (see map 3).

This overlapping of the Holy Places has been a major cause of the rivalries and conflicts which have been a characteristic of the Holy Land for so many centuries. An added factor over the past 50 years or so is that religious beliefs and practices have become prime elements in the growth of militant nationalism in this part of the world. Indeed so violent, so intense, have been the passions and emotions that have been aroused that it can be said that possession of the city and its Holy Places by any one of the three faiths will be contested by the other two. And that is what is happening now.

---

[1] For general background on the Holy Places, see Father Eugene Hoade, *Guide to the Holy Land*; Hollis and Brownrigg, *Holy Places*; Khalidi, *Jerusalem, the Arab Case*; Matthews, *Palestine, Mohammedan Holy Land*; Moore, *The Ancient Churches of Old Jerusalem*; Perowne, *The One Remains*, and *The Pilgrim's Companion in Jerusalem and Bethlehem*; Pfaff, *Jerusalem: Keystone of an Arab-Israeli Settlement*; Rackauskas, *The Internationalization of Jerusalem*; United Nations Special Committee on Palestine, *Report*, 1947; and Williams, *The Holy City*.

118

This aspect of the problem has been noted by many observers. Count Bernadotte tells us in his memoirs that when passing through Paris in 1948 on his way to take up the position of United Nations Mediator in Palestine he had a talk with French Foreign Minister Georges Bidault. He asked Bidault what would be the result if Jerusalem were to be given to the Arabs. Bidault replied that the entire Christian world would launch a new Crusade to prevent this.[2] And just two years earlier the Anglo-American Committee of Inquiry had pointed out, in words that apply just as much to Jerusalem as to the whole country, that Palestine "is not, and can never become, a land which any . . . religion can justly claim as its very own."[3]

The conflict over the Holy Places is not new: one has only to think of the Crusades, when the Christians, upon taking Jerusalem, put to the sword every Muslim and Jewish inhabitant, and then for the hundred-odd years that they ruled the city denied access to all Muslims and Jews. Students of history will recall that the Crimean War had its immediate origins in a dispute between France and Russia over protection of the Christian shrines in the Holy Land. Indeed, the French claim to a protectorate over the shrines goes back to Charlemagne, who in the VIIIth Century negotiated an agreement to this effect with the Caliph Harun al-Rashid. For many years, while the Latins, or Roman Catholics, had the support of France for their claims to certain sites, the rival claims of the Greek Orthodox were supported by Russia. In 1757, the Turkish rulers of the Holy Land sought, without complete success, to resolve the conflict between the Christian sects by issuing a *firman*, or Imperial decree, dividing the principal Christian sites between them. This led to the establishment of the so-called régime of the *status quo* governing the Holy Places (Muslim and Jewish as well as Christian), which was confirmed by another *firman* in 1852 and which with some modifications is still in effect. The *status quo* (which covers both ownership and use of the sites) formed the basis for abortive British efforts throughout the period of the Mandate to find a satisfactory solution to the problem, but none was forthcoming. This was because of the dissensions and jealousies both among Christians, Muslims and Jews and among the different Christian sects. Indeed, so great were these conflicts that the British were never able to set up a Commission for the Holy Places as provided in the Mandate. The *status quo* continued in effect, and after the 1948

[2] Bernadotte, Folke: *To Jerusalem*, p. 12.
[3] *Report* of the Anglo-American Committee of Inquiry, p. 4.

war was applied by both Israel and Jordan to the Holy Places under their respective control.

Examples of the kind of problems that arose are the conflict between Muslims and Jews over the Wailing Wall, and that between the Christian communities at the Church of the Holy Sepulchre and the Church of the Nativity. As early as 1920 there were incidents at the Wailing Wall. Ever since Byzantine times, the right of the Jews to pray at the Wall had been recognized but the British immediately found themselves presented with various problems of interpretation of the *status quo.* These included the question whether the Jews could bring with them benches or chairs when they came to worship, or whether this represented an encroachment on the rights of the Muslims, who claimed that their community owned the Wall and the pavement in front of it. (It will be recalled that the Wall is in fact the outer wall of the Haram al-Sharif.) On occasion serious rioting broke out at the Wall, notably in 1929. This led to the appointment by the British government of a commission which examined the problem and ruled that the Muslims had proprietary rights to the Wall and pavement but that the Jews had the right of access to the Wall at all times. For the remainder of the Mandate period this was the rule but regrettably the British example was not followed during the subsequent 19 years of Jordanian occupation of the Old City when the Jews were denied access to the Wall.

Disputes between the Christian sects have been a feature of the Jerusalem scene for centuries. The principal points of conflict have been the Church of the Holy Sepulchre and the Church of the Nativity. At the Holy Sepulchre, there are three major communities involved (the Latins, or Roman Catholics, the Greek Orthodox, and the Armenian Orthodox) as well as three minor ones, whose rights are minimal and whose activities are jealously watched by the first three. Certain parts of the building are recognized as the common property of the three major sects and certain other portions are allocated to one or the other of them while still others are in dispute. In the past, pitched battles have often broken out in the Church between the different clerics involved. As recently as Eastertime of 1967, there was a near riot there between two minor sects, with several people injured by flying stones, some thrown by the bishops or other leaders. It was because the squabbling between the sects in this Church was so fierce that the Turks always stationed a Muslim doorkeeper there to maintain order.

With this background, it was not surprising that when the Church of the Holy Sepulchre (damaged by an earthquake in 1927 and for many years propped up by scaffolding) was found to be in danger of collapse, it took seven years of tortuous negotiations, from 1954 to 1961, to obtain agreement among the three major communities, Latin, Greek and Armenian, to carry out the necessary repairs. This work was still under way when the June War broke out.

At the Church of the Nativity in Bethlehem, the same three sects have the major interest, but the Greek Orthodox Patriarch regards himself as being *primus inter pares*. Thus it was that during the entire three years of my tour in Jerusalem, the Dumbarton Oaks Foundation from Washington was unable to make any headway with a proposal which it had put forward for the cleaning of the mosaics in the Church. This cleaning was badly needed: the mosaics have become all but indistinguishable under the grime and smoke of centuries, so that it is impossible to examine them thoroughly or even to determine their date. The project, however, hung fire for the reason that the Greek Orthodox Patriarch, with whom I discussed the matter several times in behalf of Dumbarton Oaks, was suspicious of the fact that the latter had approached the other two Patriarchs as well as himself.

Many complications have arisen from the fact that the Church at Bethlehem encloses an Armenian Church or Chapel in the north arm of the apse. The most meticulous regulations have been prescribed for the cleaning of this chapel. For example, the Orthodox, who insist on doing the cleaning, are allowed to place a ladder on the floor of the chapel but not to lean it against the wall. This is because the carrying out of such operations as the cleaning or repair of a Holy Place can be interpreted as implying the right of exclusive possession of the portion of the building in question. The same problems have come up at the Church of the Holy Sepulchre and elsewhere. In fact, the various communities exercise their rights and claims to the different Holy Places largely by asserting the right to repair, to clean, or even to hang lamps or pictures on certain pillars or walls. This latter action is regarded as being of capital importance as it implies the exclusive possession of the wall or pillar on which the object is hung.[4]

These examples are not adduced as quaint vignettes of history or to justify any particular claim but to reinforce the fact that the conflicts over the Holy Places are so deep-seated as to make it unwise to entrust the sites to the sole care of those immediately involved. My own belief

---

[4] Details of the *status quo* and of ecclesiastical rivalries are given in Hoade, *op. cit.*, Rackauskas, *op. cit.*, and the *Memoirs* of Sir Ronald Storrs.

that some outside presence is required is enhanced by the fact that today the Jews, the Christians and the Muslims all have cause for concern at infringements of their rights in the past and possible infringements in the future.

The Jews are concerned at the denial to them for nineteen years of access to the Wailing Wall and other Jewish shrines in the Old City. They consider that their right of access was reaffirmed in the 1949 Armistice Agreement between Israel and Jordan, as in fact it seems to have been, although the language of the pertinent article of the Agreement (Article 8) is ambiguous (see Chapter V). They are also distressed at the desecration which undoubtedly took place, during the Jordanian occupation, of the Jewish cemeteries on the Mount of Olives. We ourselves had knowledge of this not only from what we observed prior to the June War, such as the bulldozing of certain graves near the so-called Tomb of Absalom to make a parking lot, but from the accounts of Israeli friends who went back to their family graves after the war and found them in a sad state. The fact that a picture taken in 1921 shows that even then the Jewish cemeteries were in great disrepair does not detract from the reality of ill-treatment at the hands of the Arabs, going so far in some cases as the use of tombstones in latrines. The Jews also are unhappy about the condition of many houses and historic synagogues in the Jewish Quarter of the Walled City, though most of this damage appears to have occurred during the heavy fighting which took place in 1948 before they were forced to evacuate the quarter.[5]

The Christians, for their part, in the period leading up to the war, were angry at their treatment at the hands of both the Muslim Jordanians and the Israelis. In Jordan, a new education law, by its requirement that all children were to be taught the religion of their parents, no matter what school they were attending, had the effect of forcing the Christian schools to teach Islam to their Muslim pupils, generally a majority. The law also contained provisions regarding textbooks and curricula that were so rigid as virtually to eliminate the possibility of teaching any material that was outside the narrow scope of Islamic lore. There were instances of discrimination against Christians in employment, and altogether the atmosphere was such as to prompt many of them to leave the country.

An incident which took place at the time of the visit of the Pope to Jerusalem in early 1964 was disturbing to the Christians. The King

---

[5] Instances of desecration of Jewish sites are given in United Nations Security Council document S/8439/add. 1., March 1, 1968.

presented to the Pope a small piece of land outside Jerusalem, on which a church was to be built. Even before this gift became public knowledge, however, a tiny mosque was hastily put up overnight on this plot of land, thus effectively blocking the project, as no mosque can ever be torn down.

In Israel, the Christians were not happy with the fact that their affairs were handled by a Ministry controlled by Orthodox Jews (the Ministry of Religious Affairs) or that the government was far from enthusiastic about church activities, particularly in the field of education. The Christians encountered various bureaucratic obstacles, such as difficulties in obtaining entry visas for new or replacement personnel for establishments that had long been in operation. On a visit to Bayt Jamal in the coastal plain, where there is an agricultural school run by the Salesian Fathers, we were told that they were allowed to bring in a new priest only when one had died. As a result of pressures of various types, in fact, most of the Christian schools in the country closed. The fact that Israeli schools and social welfare organizations have taken over most of the local services provided by Christian establishments in the past does not foreclose the need for the Christian schools, monasteries and convents to continue maintaining a Christian presence in the Holy Land.

In the New City there were instances of vandalism committed against Christian property, such as the American Protestant Cemetery, which was repeatedly broken into during the years we lived in Jerusalem. When the new Israel Museum was built on a hillside immediately adjoining the Crusader Monastery of the Cross, there was talk on the part of the Israeli authorities of taking over the Monastery and adding it to the Museum complex, as a public monument, not a religious institution. This was disturbing, as had been the earlier offer of the Israeli government to clean the Monastery, which the Greek Orthodox Patriarch, who controls the building, had refused on the grounds that under the *status quo* this would have given the Israeli government the right of ownership.

An incident which took place in the spring of 1967 and which involved the denial of access to a Christian Holy Place in Israeli-held Jerusalem was even more disturbing. This concerned Mount Zion, site of the Cenacle, or Room of the Last Supper, and of the Tomb of David. In early 1967 the Israel Ministry of Religious Affairs announced that Mount Zion would henceforth be closed on the Sabbath. This meant that Christian visitors were prevented from visiting the Cenacle on Saturdays. More alarmingly, the Israelis let it be known that there were plans to open a newly-discovered tomb, reportedly that of Solomon, in a chamber immediately adjoining the Cenacle. This would have turned the Room of the Last Supper into an anteroom for a non-Christian shrine and in the opinion of Christian authorities in Jerusalem would have produced an impossible situation. Fortunately the protests of the Christian community led to the reopening of the site on Saturdays (for Christian visitors) and the plan for opening a new tomb was dropped.

In the period just before the June War, an instance of what appeared to be religious harrassment directed by Muslims against both Christians and Jews occurred in the Old City. Very close to our Old City Consulate, and right on the edge of the no-man's land, stands a small mosque where suddenly a new public address system was installed that sent the call of the *muezzin* reverberating loudly all over the adjacent area. This occurred several times during the day and night and so great was the noise that all conversation had to be suspended while it lasted. The curious thing about this was that there were very few if any Muslim residents of this particular part of the city, which was inhabited almost entirely by Christians, at the Dominican *Ecole Biblique*, the Franciscan Sisters' Convent, the YMCA, and the Anglican Cathedral and School. Indeed, one of our Muslim employees told me that only a handful of persons occasionally attended prayers at this mosque. Given its proximity to the various Christian centers I have mentioned, and to the Israeli sector, a few yards away across the no-man's land, we could only conclude that the loudspeaker had been put up not so much to call the faithful to worship as to impress the Muslim presence on non-Muslims nearby. We discussed this nuisance, for that is what it was, with our ecclesiastical neighbors but not one of them dared complain to the authorities. I therefore did so, pointing out to the Governor of the Old City that at night we could even hear the sound in our New City residence, a mile away, and he took steps to have it somewhat toned down.

In the period before the war, the Muslims were concerned at instances of desecration by the Israelis of Muslim shrines, notably the Mamillah Cemetery directly opposite our Consulate in the New City. In 1958 one of my predecessors reported to Washington that he had been witness to the bulldozing of Muslim tombs and the conversion of the greater part of the cemetery (which I remember well from earlier visits to the city) into a public park. This action was often deplored to me by one of our Old City friends whose ancestors had been buried there. Other Muslim sites, such as the mosque at Ain Karim, to the west of the city near the new Hadassah Hospital, used as a latrine by the residents of the neighborhood, were allowed to fall into disrepair. A mosque at Safad, in northern Israel, was converted into an artists' center. In early 1967 Mayor Teddy Kollek told me that he planned to clean up the Ain Karim mosque but was encountering opposition from Orthodox elements in the Ministry of Religions; in any event the project was delayed.

While the events of the June War have naturally brought relief to the anxieties of the Jews of the world, since the Jewish Holy Places throughout the Jerusalem area are now under Israeli control, the exact opposite is true of the Muslims and Christians. Not only did the behavior of Israeli tourists in the mosques and churches of the Old City give rise to concern in the period after the opening up of the city, but there were other things that caused alarm to the Muslims and Christians. The Chief Chaplain of the Israel Defense Forces, Rabbi (Brigadier General) Goren, conducted prayers at the Haram al-Sharif itself, and the Minister of Religious Affairs spoke in an address of rebuilding the Temple on this site. The Christians and Muslims were also concerned at the falling off in the pilgrimage traffic. Tourism had been an important source of revenue before the war. In addition, a pilgrimage to the Holy Places, for the Christian and Muslim believer no less than for the Jewish, represents one of the highest manifestations of piety, and has done so ever since the medieval "palmers" made the long and perilous journey to the Holy Land and back to Europe. It soon became clear that, regardless of the assurances given by the Israeli authorities with respect to freedom of access, Christian and Muslim visitors from most foreign countries were simply not coming to the Holy Places. Under present circumstances it is hardly to be expected that, say, a Muslim from Saudi Arabia or a Christian Arab from Lebanon would visit Jerusalem—for political reasons, because all of the city is in Israeli hands.

There have been other developments that have caused concern. After the war Christian authorities who had been unable for many years to visit certain Christian properties on Mount Zion, either because they were in the no-man's land or were closed off by the Israeli military, found that some of these institutions had suffered severely. The tombs of the Armenian Patriarchs, in the courtyard of the Armenian Church of St. Savior, had been broken into and the bones scattered about. A famous mosaic floor had been removed from the church during or just after the war, and the church itself was in a deplorable state of disrepair. Several Christian cemeteries in the vicinity were in bad condition, with thick vegetation and opened graves (when my wife and I first visited Mount Zion in 1964, our Christian driver tried to locate his family graves in the Greek Orthodox cemetery but was allowed only to look through the dilapidated gate at the tangled confusion and broken stones inside). There is reason to believe, moreover, that this vandalism (which seems to result from individual acts not adequately restrained by official policy) is continuing. It was found in the spring of 1968, after the war, that the crosses on 83 tombs in the Catholic cemetery on Mount Zion had been shattered.[6] It was in this area also that the tower of the Dormition Abbey was used for many years as an Israeli machine gun nest.

Because of these developments, it is my belief that the Christians and Muslims of the world will not acquiesce indefinitely in Israeli occupation of the Holy Places and control of all means of access thereto. The example of the nineteen years when the Muslims refused to grant access to the Jews should not be repeated in reverse form. For the unique problems of Jerusalem are international, transcending purely local issues. While the city is relatively small in size and population, its influence is worldwide: it has a constituency of nearly one and a half billion persons—the 977,000,000 Christians, 474,000,000 Muslims, and 13,000,000 Jews of the world.[7]

Already some voices are being raised in protest. The Executive Committee of the National Council of Churches has gone on record in favor of an "international presence" in Jerusalem. The Vatican, whose support of internationalization was made manifest in two Papal encyclicals before the June War, has since the war reaffirmed its support for this type of solution. So has the Greek Catholic Patriarch of Antioch and the East. And Muslim opinion, in the person of King Faysal of Saudi Arabia and Inamullah Khan, Secretary General of the World Muslim Congress, has made it plain that the existing situation is not acceptable.[8] As the Greek Catholic Patriarch has pointed out, it is unfortunate that not more Christians have come forward to

[6] Instances of desecration of Christian properties in Israel are given in United Nations Security Council document S/8552, (also issued as A/7084) April 19, 1968, and in "Desecration in the Holy City" by Michael Scott, in Middle East Newsletter, August-September 1968, Vol. II, No. 7.

[7] Figures taken from the 1969 World Almanac.

[8] Views of the National Council of Churches are given in the Resolution on the Crisis in the Middle East, adopted by the Executive Committee of the Council, July 7, 1967; Vatican views are given in Rackauskas, The Internationalization of Jerusalem and Khouri, The Arab-Israel Dilemma; views of the Greek Catholic Patriarch are given in The Arab World, July-August, 1968, Vol. XIV, no. 7-8; and Muslim views are given in Khouri, op. cit.

state their views. Perhaps a factor here is the distaste which overwhelms many Western Christian visitors to the Holy City because of the tawdriness of the shrines and the petty squabbling between the different sects. It can be anticipated, however, that the anxieties of the Christians of the world, no less than those of the Muslims, will continue to grow as long as the city and all access to it remain in the sole control of the Israelis.

VIII

The Future

Regrettably, since the June War there does not appear to have been any discernible progress toward a solution of the issues outstanding between Israel and the Arab states. The Israelis have given no sign of any change in their stated position that they will not give up any of the territory they occupied in the war until the Arabs make peace. The Arabs for their part have given no sign of any change in their stated position that Israel must first agree to withdraw from the occupied areas. The impasse is thus complete and bids fair to continue for the foreseeable future.

Meanwhile the all-too-familiar pre-war pattern of raid and reprisal, tension, instability and actual fighting has not only been restored but exacerbated. While acts of irresponsible terrorism and sabotage on the part of the Arabs are certainly to be deplored, it must be stressed that the return by the Israelis to their earlier policy of retaliation has done much to set back the prospects for an accommodation between the two sides. While "an eye for an eye and a tooth for a tooth"—or rather, in Prime Minister Golda Meir's words, "seven blows for one blow"— may have worked in Canaanite times, it is a dangerous game to play in the nuclear age. Meanwhile, Israeli defense and security expenditures continue to mount.

There are two other factors which combine to make the present outlook so unfavorable. The continuing lack of any progress toward a solution of the problem of the Arab refugees has a very distinct connection with the continuance, indeed the increase, of Arab commando activity. It is among the discontented, fatalistically inclined Palestinians that the commando movement has its greatest support, since the lack of practical movement toward a settlement of the refugee problem makes them desperate and inclines their sympathies toward the activist elements. In addition, certain statements by Israeli leaders since the war have aroused great anxiety in Arab circles and have caused the

Arabs of the Old City and the West Bank to wonder just what Israeli intentions are toward them.

Immediately after the war, General Moshe Dayan said (on the television program, "Face the Nation") that Israel did not want to keep the million Arabs of the West Bank as this would turn Israel into a bi-national rather than a Jewish state, but he added that he did not think Israel should give the West Bank back to King Husayn, either. Did this not in effect mean that the Arab inhabitants would be expelled? In August 1967 the then Israeli Minister of Labor, Yigal Allon, said "The Eastern frontier of Israel passes through the middle of the Dead Sea and the River Jordan. . . . We must face the fact of the increasing birthrate among the Arabs and the necessity for them to remain a minority in Israel. We must populate the West Bank with Jewish towns and villages."

This theme of settling Jews in the occupied areas has recurred on a number of occasions. In July 1967 former Prime Minister Ben Gurion who, immediately following the war, had proposed that the walls of the Old City be razed as being a vestige of the Turkish, not the Israelite era, was quoted as saying "We have to colonize Jerusalem and its outskirts." And the then Director of Operations of the Israel Defense Forces, General Ezer Weizmann, said early in 1968 "We shall stay where we are and bring in Jews."

The idea that the Jordan River is the border of Israel was put forward on several occasions by the late Prime Minister Eshkol, notably in September 1967, in February 1968, and in his February, 1969 interview in *Newsweek*. Sometimes he called the river a "security border" and sometimes a "natural border." In August 1969, the ruling Labor Party adopted this concept as official party policy in the fall elections. A very forthright statement attributed to Dayan in the *Times* of London for June 25, 1969, went as follows:

> Our fathers had reached the frontiers which were recognized in the Partition Plan. Our generation reached the frontiers of 1949. Now the Six-Day Generation has managed to reach Suez, Jordan, and the Golan Heights. This is not the end. After the present cease-fire lines, there will be new ones. They will extend beyond Jordan—perhaps to Lebanon, and perhaps to central Syria as well.

A religious note was sounded by the Sephardic Chief Rabbi, who in the fall of 1967 was quoted as declaring that "It is forbidden by the *Torah* for all Jews, including the Israeli Government, to return even one inch of the territory of *Eretz Israel* now in our hands" (the mystical significance of the term "Eretz Israel" was pointed out in Chapter VI).

The tendency of some Israelis to hark back to Biblical prophecies describing a far vaster area as the patrimony of the Jews has done nothing to reassure the Arabs—one being from *Joshua*, I, 4, which reads:

> From the wilderness and this Lebanon, even unto the great river, the river Euphrates, all the land of the Hittites, and unto the great sea toward the going down of the sun, shall be your coast.

From the beginning of the occupation of the Old City, Israeli spokesmen have asserted that the problem of Jerusalem was not negotiable. The theme of the "unity of Jerusalem" was stressed by Foreign Minister Eban shortly after hostilities, was reiterated by Mayor Teddy Kollek on the occasion of bringing the city under Israeli municipal administration, and has been reaffirmed often since that time.

In Jerusalem, moreover, it is not only the words of the Israelis that have been disturbing to the Arabs, it is also Israeli deeds, which seem to indicate a steady strengthening of the Israeli hold over the Old City. The Arabs have assailed these actions as a violation of international law governing the administration of areas occupied as a result of hostilities.

Some 3,000 Arab residents of the former Jewish Quarter of the Walled City have been expelled from their homes, and land in this area has been expropriated. In the newer portions of the Jordanian sector to the north of the Walled City over 800 acres were also taken over. It was stated that the purpose of these expropriations was to provide for Jewish settlement. Apparently there would be a chain of new multiple housing units, linking the New City with Mount Scopus and cutting the modern Arab-inhabited area in two. The press has reported that the aim is to provide housing for 100,000 Jews. The High Rabbinical Court was moved into a Muslim girls' school in the Walled City, which was a *waqf*. An Israeli government department— the Ministry of Police—was moved into a new hospital that had been approaching completion by the Jordanians when war broke out. Following an incident near the Wailing Wall in June 1969, further evictions were carried out, and additional *waqf* property, reportedly including a mosque, was taken over. An elaborate plan for a "Jerusalem park" in the area immediately adjoining the city wall was announced. Legislation passed by the Israeli *Knesset* in August 1968 provided for the registration with the Israeli authorities of business and professional men in the Old City.

Meanwhile, arrests and deportations of Old City residents for anti-régime activities have continued, as have protest strikes, curfews and shooting incidents. More and more people have been refusing to collaborate with the Israelis for fear of reprisals. Hopes that had been raised at the time the city was opened up that the Jewish and Arab inhabitants would intermingle freely have not been realized and most Arab residents of the Old City are hesitant to go over to the New City. Those who do so are mostly menial laborers.

In the economic field, the Arab banks are still closed and unemployment remains high. Business is stagnant and the tourist trade languishing as far as Old City hotel keepers, guides, and taxi and bus drivers are concerned. Virtually no Muslim pilgrims and very few Christian pilgrims have been coming to Jerusalem. Hospitals have few patients and schools have few pupils. And yet, if a shopkeeper or businessman closes down his business and moves to the East Bank, his business is seized at once under the Israeli "absentee" law. He cannot return to Jerusalem; the 14,000 Arabs whom the Israelis have allowed to return from the East Bank since the war have almost without exception been from other parts of the occupied area. And the more time drags on and the more the Old City is incorporated administratively and economically into the Israeli scheme of things, the harder will the process be to reverse. These developments were deplored by the US Representative to the United Nations in the Security Council on July 1, 1969 (see appendix J).

While the present picture (both overall and in Jerusalem) is thus a somber one and while there has been a hardening of positions on both sides, it is clear that the present deadlock cannot go on forever. The stakes are too high, both in terms of a resolution of the underlying issues and in terms of the need to resolve the present unsatisfactory situation with respect to the city, which is of unique importance worldwide not only for its Holy Places but also for its historical and archaeological associations. It might even turn out that a settlement of the Jerusalem question could prove to be the key that would open the way to a settlement of the broader issues. Therefore let us first explore the possible solutions as far as a resolution of the Jerusalem problem is concerned.

A basic assumption underlying any solution for Jerusalem is that most if not all of the West Bank would be returned to Jordanian, or at least to Arab, control. If Israel is to remain in indefinite occupation of the West Bank there is hardly any point in discussing any change in the present status aside from remarking that the result will be to sow the seeds of a future war. If, on the other hand, some arrangement can be worked out for a substantial Israeli withdrawal from the West Bank, the question of Jerusalem will immediately arise. This is because of the close links between the West Bank and the Old City, to say nothing of the broader issues involved. While hopefully there would be no return to the barbed wire, the barricades and the land mines of 1948-1967, any solution for Jerusalem should cover the following points: Jordanian and Israeli interests in the city, and the interests of the Arab and Jewish inhabitants, would need to be protected; free access to all the Holy Places would need to be guaranteed for all pilgrims and other visitors; and there would need to be full recognition of the international interest in the city.

By recognition of the international interest is meant not only the interest of the Christians, Jews and Muslims of the world but of the United Nations itself. The Muslim interest is not confined to Israel's immediate Arab neighbors; it will be recalled that during the 1967 crisis such relatively faraway Muslim countries as Pakistan or Morocco were vociferous in defense of Muslim rights in the Holy City. The world interest is not confined to religious issues but focusses likewise on Jerusalem's unique status as one of the great cities of the world. As regards the United Nations, it will be recalled that almost from its inception the UN has had before it the problem of Jerusalem and that the city has been the center of important United Nations activities in both the armistice and refugee fields.

By free access for all is meant to assure that members of all three faiths, or indeed any tourist, can feel free to visit Jerusalem in the sense that most Muslims and some Christians cannot do today. This is because the Arab governments, under existing circumstances, object to their citizens' going to territory under Israeli control, and returning home. Furthermore, Israeli suspicions might be aroused by large numbers of visiting Arabs.

By protection of Jordan's interest in the city is meant not only the interest of Jordanian Muslims in the Haram al-Sharif and other shrines but the economic ties between the West Bank (and also the East Bank) and the Old City. It cannot be emphasized enough that the Old City was until June 1967 the commercial center for the West Bank and an important source of revenue for Jordan through tourism.

By protection of Israel's interest is meant not only the fact that Israel has established its capital there and attaches great importance to the question of access to the Wailing Wall and other Jewish sites but also the historic ties that bind world Jewry with Jerusalem. Finally, it goes without saying that in any proposed solution the interests of the people of Jerusalem, Jewish as well as Arab, should be safeguarded.

These, then, are the assumptions on which any attempt at a solution of the Jerusalem question should be based: Jordanian return to the West Bank, no return to the barbed wire, protection of the interests of Jordan and Israel and of the residents of the city, free access, and recognition of the international interest. Let us now discuss the various alternative solutions that might be put forward and see how each one would meet the requirements of our basic assumptions.

1. *Continued Israeli control,* perhaps with some sort of international advisory commission to represent international religious and other interests.

It should be evident by this time that I do not consider that Christian and Muslim opinion, and world opinion, would be satisfied by a continuance of the present situation. Nor of course would Jordanian or Arab interests. A commission for the Holy Places would not be a sufficient safeguard, since the real issue for the Christians and the Muslims is Jewish occupation and control of their Holy Places.

2. *Return of the Old City to Jordanian control.* This alternative, while obviously acceptable to Jordanian and Arab and Muslim opinion, would be inacceptable on all other grounds. It would be impossible to get Israel and the Jews of the world to agree, after recent experiences, to put the Jewish shrines back under Jordanian control, even though the Jordanian government has offered to provide full access to the Wailing Wall and other Jewish sites if Jordan were to get back the Old City. It would probably also be hard to get Christian agreement in view of the fact that, prior to the war, the Christians were becoming increasingly unhappy with their treatment at the hands of the Muslim majority in Jordan. Finally, this solution would mean that the city would again be divided and the barbed wire brought back, an outcome that would surely be undesirable.

3. *A Condominium between Israel and Jordan.* Under this alternative, the administration of the city would be shared by the two governments. It is hard to see how this type of arrangement would be acceptable to either party, given the past history of their relationship, or how it would be workable. Israel would certainly oppose a condominium over the whole city as this would mean sharing sovereignty over the New City, where it has established its capital. Arrangements could possibly be worked out to assure free access, but a purely local solution of this kind would not provide adequate recognition of the international interest in the city.

My conclusion is that these three alternative solutions, which could all be termed local kinds of solution, are not acceptable. This would leave the different variants of internationalization. In considering these it may be well to bear in mind that now that the city is united again it should prove easier to treat it as a single entity than in the period following 1947, when the fact that the city was already physically divided between Israel and Jordan made it all but impossible to internationalize it. It should also be understood that in my view it is only through some form of internationalization that the unique character of the city can be preserved. For Jerusalem is more than just an Arab town and a Jewish town side by side: it is so timeless in its uniqueness that it is an Eternal City no less than Rome.

In Chapter VII I made the point that so violent, so intense, are the passions and emotions that have been aroused over the Holy Places that possession of the city and its shrines by any one of the three contesting faiths will be opposed by the other two, and that the Christians and Muslims of the world are not going to acquiesce indefinitely in Israeli occupation of their Holy Places. I also expressed my conviction that the conflicts that have repeatedly arisen over the Holy Places are so deep seated as to make some outside presence essential, and that the problem of Jerusalem is an international one, transcending purely local issues. For these reasons, I regard an international type of solution as essential.

There are three possible types of internationalization: full territorial internationalization, partial territorial internationalization, and functional internationalization (see appendix F).

1. *Full Territorial Internationalization* of the area included in the 1947 partition plan (the *corpus separatum*).

This solution has the advantage that it encompasses all of the Holy Places in the vicinity of Jerusalem. The area is so large, however—100 square miles with a current population of over 250,000—as to offer virtually insuperable administrative obstacles in terms of devising a form of government, as the United Nations discovered during its lengthy consideration of the Jerusalem problem. Moreover, after all the years when they divided the *corpus separatum* between them, both Israel and Jordan would certainly object to its being revived. It simply is not a practical alternative today.

2. *Partial Territorial Internationalization* of an area smaller than the *corpus separatum* of the 1947 plan, with Israel and Jordan, respectively, controlling the remainder.

This appears to be the most promising of the different alternatives, although manifestly it involves serious problems. It should, however, prove possible to identify an area, such as the Walled City and the area immediately surrounding it, which would contain the most important Holy Places but which would be sufficiently compact as to be manageable in terms of international administration. This will be discussed in further detail below.

Such a solution would make it possible to meet the requirements of the international interest and the question of access. The smaller the area to be internationalized and the greater the area left under Israeli or Jordanian administration, the less would be the problem of providing for Israeli or Jordanian interests in the internationalized area or for those of its Jewish and Arab population.

3. *Functional Internationalization* of the Holy Places only. This alternative has the advantage of avoiding any decisions of a territorial nature as well as the fact that in the past at least it has appealed to one of the parties immediately concerned (Israel). What would presumably be attempted under existing conditions would be to draw up some form of arrangement under United Nations auspices for putting the Holy Places under international protection, with full guarantees of access, while continuing to leave Israel in occupation of the whole of Jerusalem. In other words, this variant would not appear to differ in substance from the first alternative discussed above, continued Israeli control, and would be open to the same objections.

A proposal for partial territorial internationalization should, in my view, cover the Walled City of Jerusalem at the very least (see map 3). The Walled City has the advantage that it is a finite area that can be set apart readily and administered more easily than a larger area. It contains the most important shrines, notably the Wailing Wall, the Dome of the Rock, and the Church of the Holy Sepulchre. Its area as stated above is approximately one square kilometer and its population about 25,000.

There are, however, a number of shrines in the immediately surrounding area, particularly the Mount of Olives, the Garden of Gethsemane, and the Jewish tombs which lie between the Walled City and the crest of the Mount of Olives. To the immediate southwest of the Walled City stands Mount Zion, sacred to all three faiths. I would therefore suggest that Mount Zion on the one side and the Mount of Olives and the intervening area on the other be included in the proposed international sector. These, incidentally, are areas that were under the control of Israel or Jordan, respectively, before the June War, so that counterbalancing concessions by each side would be involved.

A final site that might be included in the proposed international zone would be Government House and its surrounding UN enclave, with a connecting corridor. This would involve topographical problems in view of the fact that Government House is about a mile and a half from the Walled City, but there would be psychological advantages in terms of maintaining a UN presence in the international zone. This would be all the more true if it could be arranged, as some think advisable, for some major UN unit in addition to UNTSO and UNRWA to be transferred to Jerusalem. Conceivably the UNTSO and UNRWA offices could be moved into the international zone but it might be preferable to add the UN enclave, which has been under the United Nations since 1948, to the zone.

The remaining parts of the formerly Jordanian-administered area which were incorporated into the Israeli municipality in 1967 but which would not be included in the international zone would revert to Jordanian control. It would be necessary to devise some type of corridor to provide direct access across the Jordanian-administered area to the Jewish institutions on Mount Scopus. Israel would retain the no-man's land, which it occupied in 1967, aside from such portions of the Government House enclave and contiguous territory as might be included in the international zone. With the possible exception of Mount Zion, Israel would not be asked to give up any territory formerly in the Israeli sector of Jerusalem and would thus continue to maintain its capital in the New City. This should make it possible eventually for the various embassies in Tel Aviv to be moved to the Israeli part of Jerusalem.

These suggestions are put forward as merely illustrative. The actual boundaries of the international area would, of course, be subject to negotiation. The main objective is to get recognition of the principle of internationalization. Then the precise boundaries could be determined.

Supreme authority over the international zone would rest with the United Nations, which would appoint a United Nations Administrator who would embody the UN presence in the city. Day-to-day administration would at first be entirely in the hands of the Administrator but would be progressively turned over to a City Council, elected by the residents of the zone. The Administrator would be responsible for the application of laws and the administration of justice, the preservation of order, the provision of educational, public health and postal services, the regulation of business and labor and the collection of taxes. At the outset the Administrator would be responsible for the provision of such municipal services as electricity, water, sewage, refuse collection, street cleaning and lighting, and street maintenance, but eventually the City Council would take over these functions. They could be contracted out on either the Arab or the Israeli side, depending on which could provide the better service; before the war, for example, the supply of electricity was better in the Old City and of water in the New, while the Old City street cleaning service was incomparably more effective. The City Council would be organized into committees which would focus on particular matters such as education or taxation. The Administrator would be assisted by two deputy administrators, appointed by the governments of Israel and Jordan respectively, and by an Advisory Council composed of representatives of the different religious sects and other elements having an interest in the Holy City.

The arrangements for the international zone would include a provision for both Israel and Jordan to benefit from the revenues from tourism in the zone. There would also have to be agreement with respect to taxation, judicial and currency matters and to the citizenship to be held by residents of the zone. A promising source of revenue would be a tourist tax levied on all visitors coming to the international zone from countries other than Israel or Jordan. The sale of stamps would, as in the case of Vatican City, be another source of income.

Access to all Holy Places within the wider area proposed for internationalization in 1947 would be guaranteed, by the United Nations for the international zone, and by Israel or Jordan (as the case might be) for the places under their jurisdiction. There would be the greatest possible freedom of movement between the international zone and Israel or Jordan, but each of these governments would be allowed to exercise some control over this, in order to prevent terrorist infiltration or smuggling. The Administrator would be responsible for the protection of the Holy Places within the zone (presumably with the aid of an international police force) but the actual maintenance of the sites would be in the hands of the different religious communities.

The Administrator would of course have to be selected with care. He should not be a person too closely affiliated with one of the various religious denominations having an active rôle in Jerusalem nor should he be a career official of the United Nations; this would make him unacceptable to Israel. His position would be like that of an American city manager, a professionally trained administrator.

The foregoing proposal is made in the full knowledge that Israel has declared that the Old City is going to remain in its hands and that the issue of Jerusalem is not negotiable. It is true that the Israelis have a strong card in their physical possession of the city but the Arabs also hold a strong card in that their consent is necessary for any settlement of the overall problems at issue. Israel might therefore acquiesce in a solution for Jerusalem along the foregoing lines if it were to develop that this would bring with it a permanent peace settlement, which Israel surely needs in order to remove the threat of a new war. In this manner Jerusalem could be the key to peace and indeed could truly emerge as the City of Peace which its name implies.

While this may mean that any solution for Jerusalem can only be reached as a part of an overall settlement, manifestly there would be distinct advantages if it could be reached before. Pressures now felt in Israel for complete annexation of the Old City would be warded off and the enhanced freedom of movement among the Arab and Jewish population that would follow would facilitate exchanges of all kinds and lead to greater understanding.

Advantages which Israel would gain from an early solution for Jerusalem, in addition to continuing access to the Jewish shrines, are: (1) it could retain the New City as its capital and gain international acceptance of this fact; (2) it could share in the tourist revenues, which would greatly expand over the present level, and (3) it could look to the removal of a serious source of friction with Christian and Muslim world opinion and with the world community generally.

How and when such a proposal would be put forward and how to bring in the various interested parties (not just Jordan and Israel but the wider interests, Christian, Jewish, and Muslim and the United Nations) would have to be determined. It seems likely that the two countries most immediately affected are going to require some outside assistance, and even strong pressure if they are to come to an accommodation over Jerusalem. The potential benefits to the whole world, however, as well as to the people of Jerusalem itself, are so great, if a solution to the problem of the city can be found, that I have ventured, in spite of its obvious difficulties, to put this proposal forward. In the words of the prophet Isaiah (LXII, 1): "For Zion's sake I will not hold my peace."

In conclusion I would like to offer a few comments about the wider aspects of the Arab-Israel question. It is my firm belief that there is going to have to be a fundamental change in attitude on both sides if there is to be a lasting peace in the Middle East. The Israelis will have to discard the notion, all too commonly held in Israel and a relic of Mandate days, that the Arabs are just *fallahin* (peasants) or petty merchants, to be looked down on and basically distrusted. The iron curtain which separated the two communities for nineteen years prevented the Israelis from learning about the changes that have been going on in the Arab world. They must stop trying to put the clock back to 1948 and must understand that there has grown up in the Arab countries a whole new professional and intellectual élite with whom it should be possible to work for the benefit of both communities. The failure of the Zionists to take sufficiently into account the attitude of the Arabs has been one of the great tragedies of the Palestine question over the years.

In this effort of readjustment, perhaps it will be possible for Israel's Oriental Jews, now in the majority in the country, to play some part, since their background is at least partly that of the Arab world from which they came. The same could be true of Israel's Arabs and of the million or so Arabs now living in the occupied territories, particularly if the idea which has been advanced of setting up some kind of Palestinian entity can be developed. The Palestinian Arabs have never gained the Arab state that was promised them in the 1947 partition plan. At the same time both the Jews of Palestine and the Arabs in all neighboring countries have achieved nationhood. While in any settlement they would presumably revert to some status linking them to Jordan, they should be given more autonomy than they had. They thus might serve as a bridge between the state of Israel and the Arab states, although manifestly this will depend on a lessening of the tensions which at present are inflaming the atmosphere not only in the occupied areas, but in all the Middle East.

The Arabs in general deeply resent the attitude of superiority, even arrogance, which the Israelis display toward them. This will need to be tempered, as will the unwillingness to compromise that has characterized much of Israel's outlook toward its neighbors. As General E. L. M. Burns, the former Chief of Staff of UNTSO, puts it in his book *Between Arab and Israeli:*

> It is not unreasonable to deduce that a society whose young elements have passed their most formative years in an atmosphere in which the military virtues and especially aggressiveness are given the highest values, and where the Arab is always the enemy, to be made to submit to Israel's demands by ruthless force, will grow increasingly militaristic and less inclined to the solving by negotiation of external problems. (p. 68)

The attention devoted in Israel today to the study of the Old Testament has the effect of enhancing the martial qualities mentioned by General Burns, for it is an easy transition from the wars against the

Amalekites, the Moabites, the Perrizites or the Philistines of Biblical times to the present-day concept of "Fortress Israel," surrounded by hostile Arabs.

Arab fears of Israeli expansionism must also be allayed. Many Arabs have an anti-Western outlook and it is a simple matter for a trouble maker to cast Israel in the rôle of the colonialist—the outsider whom the Western imperialists have planted in the midst of the Arab world for the purpose of extending their system over it. The Israelis should talk less in terms of Israel's being an outpost of Western civilization and more in terms of its being another Middle Eastern state. With the relative drying up of Jewish immigration and the rapid growth of the Oriental Jewish and Israeli Arab population it is becoming just that. Above all, reliance on Biblical prophecy as justifying claims to further territories must be renounced.

Naturally it is not all on one side that changes need to be made. The Arabs, too, will need to adopt an entirely new attitude. It is time for them, also, to renounce their threats to drive the Israelis into the sea and to cease reminding the world that just as their ancestors brought the Crusader Kingdom of Jerusalem to an end, so will they dispose of Israel sooner or later. While some may feel, as does the present writer, that the creation of a Jewish state in Palestine twenty-odd years ago against the wishes of the majority (two-thirds) of the inhabitants of the country was a mistake, this is not the issue today.

The issue for the Arabs is not how to get rid of Israel but how to learn to live with it, just as the issue for Israel is how to learn to live with the Arabs.

That Israel is here to stay should be obvious. The Arabs know that the powers, especially the United States, would oppose any effort to eliminate Israel. At all events, Israel has shown that it can take care of itself. After their third defeat at the hands of the Jews this should begin to sink in on the Arabs.

It will take some time for Arab opinion to change and for the atmosphere of bitterness and hatred that has enveloped the problem for so many years to dissipate. Fortunately there are some Arabs who see that the Arab states cannot go on indefinitely pursuing the same negative, sterile course. If they do, they will forfeit world sympathy and their best people, their educated classes will continue emigrating abroad rather than raising their children in hate and fear.

Once the Arabs grasp the idea that Israel is part of the Middle East and is bound to remain so, perhaps some day, instead of resenting the sums of money poured into Israel (some $200,000,000 in private funds each year from the United States alone) they will realize that this effort can be used for the benefit of the region as a whole. Such institutions supported from abroad as the Hebrew University or the Hadassah Medical Organization should serve the whole Middle East, not only Israel. And the day may even come when the Arabs begin to appreciate the very real achievements of the Israelis in so many walks of life—in building up their country, forging a nation and advancing so rapidly in technical and scientific accomplishments.

In spite of present tensions, voices are already being raised on both sides, calling for a change in basic attitudes. Some Arabs are even suggesting that they made a mistake in having as their objective the destruction of Israel. One thinks here of King Husayn of Jordan or President Bourghiba of Tunisia. Some Jews are pointing out that Muslims and Jews have much in common in their religion, their Law, that both Isaac and Ishmael were sons of Abraham. In other words, some people on both sides are looking for an accommodation of the basic issue, which is between the Jewish search for survival and the Arab search for dignity.

However, here again it would seem that outside intervention will be needed to bring the parties together. Their positions have hardened and the illusions, the myths, that each side has regarding the other, have in a sense become the realities of the situation. Each side is so firmly fixed in its position that there is little room for maneuver and it therefore seems unlikely under existing circumstances that the two parties will get together voluntarily.

Should outside pressure be brought to bear (presumably by the four Great Powers working through the United Nations), any approach to the parties should include the following: (1) a limit to the arms race along the lines of the Tripartite Declaration of 1950; (2) the orderly development of the Jordan waters along the lines of the Eric Johnston plan; and (3) the resolution of the refugee problem along the lines of the Joseph Johnson proposals (see Chapter IV for all three).

Compensation paid to the refugees should be tied to constructive projects and should not be merely in cash, which would be quickly dissipated on consumer goods. Those refugees settling on the West Bank should be assisted by Israel and Jordan to develop light industries like those in the new Israeli development towns, for example, plants for processing vegetables or fruits, and to improve their farming methods, particularly through mechanization. When we travelled about on the West Bank we were always struck by the lack of industrial development or of any modernized agriculture, by comparison with

Israel and Lebanon. The authorities in Amman seem to have avoided developing the area, out of fear of Israeli seizure—which occurred—but in the future it is capable of much modernization. Specific assistance of this type to the West Bank by Israel and Jordan would enhance the image of both countries in the eyes of the Palestinians and would serve as an inducement to them to "live at peace with their neighbors," to use the language of the 1948 United Nations resolution regarding the refugees. And since a great deal of this activity would originate in Jerusalem, here again Jerusalem could be the key — to peaceful development.

An essential feature of any attempt at a peace is that Israel must somehow be convinced that mere repression will not calm Arab fears, and the Arabs must be made to realize that terrorism will only intensify Israel's determination to take whatever steps it feels necessary for its security. In any event, true pacification will not come through continued reliance by both sides on armed force but through mutual accommodation and acceptance on both sides.

If it is true that the real partition for twenty years was in the minds of men, then it is there that the search for a lasting peace must begin. There must be a dialogue between equals, between fellow members of the same community of the Middle East.

While some of what is said above may seem visionary, it is worth recalling that Arabs and Jews have worked together before: In the days of the great Arab Empire, when Jewish scholars like Maimonides were held in high esteem; in Ottoman times, when it was not unusual for a Palestinian Arab family to adopt a Jewish boy as blood brother to its own sons; and even under the Mandate when it proved possible for some Arabs and Jews to cooperate in government and in the professions. After all, Jews, Muslims and Christians all have a common heritage in the Holy Land. It is time, after all these years of conflict, for them to make a real effort to live together in the land where they all belong. Otherwise, the Middle East faces a future of continuing violence and bloodshed, with an intensification of the arms race and with the prospect that the next conflict may be a nuclear one.

Appendix A
The McMahon Correspondence

Prior to the First World War, the Arabs had already approached the British to ask help in obtaining their independence from Turkey. Following the outbreak of war, the Sharif Husayn of Mecca, speaking for the "Arab nation," wrote a letter to the British High Commissioner in Cairo, Sir Henry McMahon, outlining the conditions on which the Arabs were prepared to enter into an alliance with the British in the war against Turkey. The letters, exchanged between Husayn and McMahon on this subject, have become known as the McMahon Correspondence.

In his first letter, dated July 14, 1915, the Sharif Husayn proposed specific boundaries for the area in which the independence of the Arabs would be recognized by the British in return for Arab entry into the war. Essentially this area was bounded on the north by a line running eastward from Mersin in Asia Minor to the Persian frontier; on the east by Persia; on the south by the Indian Ocean; and on the west by the Red Sea and the Mediterranean: in other words it encompassed roughly the Arabian Peninsula and the area to the north often called the Fertile Crescent. McMahon replied that a discussion of precise boundaries was premature but Husayn insisted that there must be agreement on the area proposed for independence as a prerequisite to Arab cooperation in the war effort. In his letter of October 24, 1915, therefore, McMahon signified British acceptance of the proposed boundaries, the following being the crucial portions of his pledge:

> The districts of Mersin and Alexandretta, and portions of Syria lying to the west of the districts of Damascus, Homs, Hama and Aleppo, cannot be said to be purely Arab, and must on that account be excepted from the proposed delimitation.
>
> Subject to that limitation . . . we accept that delimitation.
>
> As for the regions lying within the proposed frontiers, in which Great Britain is free to act without detriment to the interests of her ally, France, I am authorized to give you the following pledges on behalf of the Government of Great Britain, and to reply as follows to your note:
>
> (1) That, subject to the modifications stated above, Great Britain is prepared to recognize and uphold the independence of the Arabs in all regions lying within the frontiers proposed by the Sharif of Mecca; . . .

Later in the correspondence, the Sharif reluctantly agreed to wait until after the war before reverting to the subject of certain regions where the interests of France were said by the British to be involved, but he reiterated the Arab claim of independence for the entire area.

The wording of McMahon's pledge has been the subject of endless controversy ever since it was made. In the first place, the Arabic phraseology employed in the entire McMahon Correspondence (on both sides) was flowery and imprecise. Secondly, McMahon said what he was *excluding* from his pledge of independence but at no point in the correspondence did he say what he was *including*. (Years later, in 1937, he did state that he had not intended to have the pledge cover Palestine, but by then the damage had been done.)

143

Thirdly, while it is true that the name "Palestine" does not appear in the correspondence, it is difficult to maintain, as British spokesmen have sometimes tried
to do, that Palestine could be regarded as lying "west of the districts of Damascus,
Homs, Hama and Aleppo," and hence as coming within the area reserved by
McMahon.

It should be remembered that the time the pledge was extended by McMahon,
the British were in a critical phase insofar as the war with Turkey was concerned, so much so that London instructed McMahon to make every effort to
gain Arab support. They thus were focussing primarily on this objective.

Subsequently, the Arabs received assurances as to their future independence
which were categorical and seemingly unequivocal. In January 1918, that is,
after the issuance of the Balfour Declaration and the revelation of the Sykes-
Picot Agreement, and after the publication of Woodrow Wilson's Fourteen
Points, the British government sent an envoy to assure the Sharif Husayn of
Mecca that "Jewish settlement in Palestine would only be allowed in so far as
would be consistent with the political and economic freedom of the Arab
population." Later in the same year the British Arab Bureau in Cairo, in a
statement delivered to seven Arab leaders and hence known as the "Declaration
to the Seven," asserted that with regard to the former Turkish territories
occupied by the Allied Armies it was the policy of the British government that
"the future government of these territories should be based upon the principle of
the consent of the governed." And on November 7, 1918, an official com-
muniqué, known as the Anglo-French Proclamation since it outlined the policy
of both the British and French governments in the liberated areas, was issued by
the British military authorities in Iraq, Syria and Palestine. It stated that the
aim of the Allies was "the setting up of national governments . . . that shall
derive their authority from the free exercise of the initiative and choice of the
indigenous populations." The language used suggests that the postwar settlement, at least insofar as Palestine was concerned, was more incompatible with
these three statements of policy than with the less precise wording employed in
the McMahon Correspondence.

As a final comment on the correspondence, it should be pointed out that after
the war the French concurred in the assumption by the British of the sole
responsibility for Palestine, which thus became, in the language of Sir Henry
McMahon's note, a region where Great Britain was "free to act without
detriment to the interests of her ally France." This reinforced the view of the
Arabs that Palestine was a part of the area where Arab independence would be
recognized.

Sources: The McMahon Correspondence was not published by the British government until the Palestine Round Table Conference of 1939 when it was made public
as *Command Paper no. 5974*. The correspondence, however, appeared the previous
year as an appendix to Antonius' *The Arab Awakening*. It may also be found in
Hurewitz, *Diplomacy in the Near and Middle East*. The January 1918 pledge to
Husayn, the Declaration to the Seven and the Anglo-French Proclamation are also
in Antonius and Hurewitz.

For a discussion of the background and implications, see, in addition to Antonius,
Jeffries' *Palestine, the Reality*, Howard, *The King-Crane Commission*, and Monroe,
Britain's Moment in the Middle East. Antonius' book contains a map of the area
claimed by the Arabs.

Appendix B
The Balfour Declaration

Throughout the centuries since the Dispersion in 70 A. D., the Jewish people had maintained an abiding interest in the land where Judaism had been born. With a few intervals there had almost continuously been colonies of religious Jews in the country, mainly in the holy cities of Jerusalem, Tiberias, Safad and Hebron. In the late nineteenth century, as a result of the 1881 pogroms in Russia and the anti-Semitic overtones of the 1894 Dreyfus case in France, there began to develop among some European Jews a conviction that the Jews had to have a state of their own. It was the Viennese journalist Theodor Herzl, who had covered the Dreyfus trial and had been appalled at the extent of the anti-Semitism that he observed there, who furnished the main inspiration for the Zionist movement.

In his book, *Der Judenstaat* (The Jewish State), 1896, Herzl argued that the Jewish question was essentially a nationalist question, not a religious one, and that the answer was a Jewish State. While at one point in his book he mentions Palestine, he does not appear to have been convinced that the Jewish state necessarily had to be in that country. It is true that the first Zionist Congress, held at Basle in 1897, under Herzl's leadership, resolved that the aim of the movement was "to create for the Jewish people a home in Palestine secured by public law." Herzl's major interest, however, seems to have been focussed on the words "secured by public law," since it was his conviction that the Jewish state, wherever located—and among his first choices was Argentina—should have its existence guaranteed by the Great Powers. Herzl also thought that the governments of the countries where anti-Semitism was prevalent would welcome the concept of a Jewish state and would work actively for its implementation.

In negotiations with British Colonial Secretary Joseph Chamberlain, Herzl secured the offer of a tract of land in Uganda (more accurately, in what is now Kenya), which was to be known as "New Palestine." This offer was debated at the Sixth Zionist Congress in 1903. Herzl argued for acceptance of the British offer, but it became clear that the Eastern European Zionists, led by Menahem Ussishkin and Chaim Weizmann, who were insistent upon Palestine, were in the ascendant. Herzl died the next year and the movement came increasingly under the influence of Weizmann, who moved to England at about that time and whose first meeting with Arthur James Balfour was in 1906.

Following the outbreak of the First World War, the Zionists in Great Britain held a series of discussions with leaders of the British government regarding the future of Palestine and the possibility of a British declaration of support for their aims. The idea that it might be possible to capitalize upon the Jewish connec-

145

tion with Palestine to secure strategic advantages for Great Britain was not new
—it had been advanced by Lord Palmerston as far back as 1840. The British
were well aware of the influence which Jews had in certain countries, notably
the United States, where one of President Wilson's close advisers was Justice
Louis D. Brandeis, a firm supporter of the Zionist cause. The British government was also fearful that the Germans, in an attempt to secure Jewish support,
might issue some statement of their own in support of Zionist aspirations. It
thus appeared that there were advantages in a British statement along these lines
such as the Zionist leaders were requesting. It is sometimes claimed that the
government was also motivated by a desire to reward Weizmann (who was a
chemist) for his work in the production of acetone, an ingredient of smokeless
powder, but this does not appear to have been an important consideration and
in any event Weizmann tells us in his memoirs that he received a bonus of ten
thousand pounds for his work.

On the other hand, there was considerable anti-Zionist sentiment among the
Jews of Great Britain and other countries. Many feared that if a Jewish state
was established, all the Jews of the world would be expected to go there.
Indeed, the opposition in the Cabinet was led by Edwin Montagu, Secretary of
State for India, who was a confirmed anti-Zionist and the only Jew in Cabinet.

In July 1917 the President of the Zionist Federation of Great Britain, Lord
Rothschild, submitted to the government a draft declaration which would have
provided that Palestine should be "recognized as the National Home of the
Jewish People." (Later the word "recognized" was changed to "reconstituted.")
After considerable delay, Balfour on November 2, 1917, wrote to Lord
Rothschild as follows:

> I have much pleasure in conveying to you, on behalf of His Majesty's Govern-
> ment, the following declaration of sympathy with Jewish Zionist aspirations
> which has been submitted to, and approved by the Cabinet.
>
> His Majesty's Government view with favor the establishment in Palestine of a
> national home for the Jewish people, and will use their best endeavors to facilitate
> the achievement of this object, it being clearly understood that nothing shall be
> done which may prejudice the civil and religious rights of existing non-Jewish
> communities in Palestine, or the rights and political status enjoyed by Jews in
> any other country.
>
> I should be grateful if you would bring this declaration to the knowledge of the
> Zionist Federation.

Prior to the issuance of the Balfour Declaration the text was approved by
President Wilson and subsequently the French and Italian governments gave
the Declaration their general endorsement.

The Balfour Declaration, with its apparently deliberately ambiguous wording,
is a curious document. Its affirmation of support for the establishment "in
Palestine" of a Jewish national home (lower case) without any further amplifi-
cation is in marked contrast to the Zionist proposal that Palestine be made *the*
National Home (in capitals) of the Jewish People. Interestingly enough, the
two safeguarding clauses which the Cabinet added, pertaining to the rights of
the non-Jewish population and of Jews elsewhere, are stated in more positive
terms than the main clause regarding the National Home. The "civil and
religious rights" of the non-Jewish inhabitants are not defined, nor is there any
mention of their "political status" as compared with that of the Jews in other

countries. Even the use of the expression "in Palestine" is lacking in precision, since at that time there was no area clearly defined as such. The characterization of the Arabs of Palestine as "the existing non-Jewish communities" is remarkable since this element accounted for some 91 percent of the population at that time—a fact little appreciated, particularly on the part of the Zionists (the word "Arab" does not appear in Herzl's *Judenstaat*, and it is said that Herzl himself expressed great surprise on being informed of their existence).

It seems clear that the Balfour Declaration was drafted in such a way as to make it susceptible to varying interpretations, as indeed it has been by British spokesmen over the years. Moreover, the use of the phrase "national home" in both the Zionist text and the final text is a reflection of the fact that at the time the Zionists themselves were not sure of what their objective was, and were in any event anxious not to alienate anti-Zionist opinion.

As for Balfour himself, it emerges, from a recently published letter which he wrote Sir Alfred Zimmern under date of September 19, 1918, (*Middle East Journal*, Summer, 1968, p. 343) that he was in favor of an eventual Jewish state in Palestine. There was also the significant statement attributed to him by Marlowe (*The Seat of Pilate*, 1959), that "in Palestine we do not propose ever to go through the form of consulting . . . the present inhabitants." Indeed the Balfour Declaration was not made public in Palestine itself for two and a half years.

In retrospect, it would appear that the eventual aim of the Zionists was to gain control of Palestine and establish a Jewish majority there, Weizmann's statement at Paris in 1919, that they wanted to make it "as Jewish as England is English" bears this out. This was also the thrust of Lloyd George's 1936 statement to the Peel Commission, to the effect that the intention was that if the Jews responded to the opportunity afforded them to come to Palestine and establish a majority there, it would become a Jewish state. It is interesting also that the early discussions of the matter in the British War Cabinet were in terms of a Jewish state.

Sources: The text of the Balfour Declaration may be found in Hurewitz' *Diplomacy in the Near and Middle East* and in many other sources. The literature regarding the Declaration is voluminous. The most important works are undoubtedly Stein's *The Balfour Declaration* and Weizmann's memoirs (*Trial and Error*). Two basic works written from the Jewish standpoint are Halpern, *The Idea of the Jewish State*, and Hertzberg (ed.) *The Zionist Idea*; and from the Arab standpoint, Antonius' *The Arab Awakening* and Jeffries' *Palestine, the Reality*. Other useful background material can be found in Khouri, *The Arab-Israeli Dilemma*, Walter Z. Laqueur, *The Road to Jerusalem*, Elizabeth Monroe, *Britain's Moment in the Middle East*, Christopher Sykes, *Two Studies in Virtue* and *Crossroads to Israel*, and Barbara Tuchman, *Bible and Sword.*

Appendix C
The Sykes-Picot Agreement

As soon as the British had concluded their negotiations with the Sharif of Mecca (in the McMahon Correspondence) they proposed to the French that the two governments should hold discussions regarding Syria (where the French had a claim going back many years) and other parts of the Ottoman Empire. These discussions were carried out in late 1915 and early 1916 by Sir Mark Sykes, of the British Foreign Office, who was serving as Chief Secretary to the War Cabinet, and Georges Picot, former French Consul General in Beirut. In March 1916 Sykes and Picot went to Petrograd and held talks with the Russian government. The three powers then exchanged diplomatic notes in which the claims of each of the three to certain Turkish territories were outlined and were recognized by the other two. It is these notes which constitute the Sykes-Picot Agreement. In 1917 Italy, which had laid claim to portions of Asia Minor, was included in the agreement through negotiations which took place at St. Jean de Maurienne.

The Sykes-Picot Agreement could hardly be farther from the "open covenants of peace openly arrived at" stressed by Woodrow Wilson in his Fourteen Points. Among other provisions, Russia was to get Constantinople, and France and Great Britain were to divide Syria and Iraq. With respect to Palestine, which was referred to as the "Brown area," the Anglo-French exchange of notes provided that:

> In the Brown area there shall be established an international administration of which the form shall be decided upon after consultation with Russia, and after subsequent agreement with the other Allies and the representatives of the Sharif of Mecca.

The British were also to be given the ports of Haifa and Acre, in Palestine, and were to construct a railway from Haifa eastward to their zone.

During the negotiations the French first put in a claim to the whole of Syria, including Palestine. This the British countered by proposing that Palestine should be subject to a special international régime. Ostensibly this was because of the Holy Places but actually the intent was to deny the French any exclusive control over Palestine, to which British strategists attached considerable importance because of its proximity to the Suez Canal. The French then suggested that the international régime apply only to Jerusalem and Bethlehem and their immediate environs (a forerunner, incidentally, of the 1947 United Nations partition plan), while the rest of Palestine would be considered a part of Syria. However, when Sykes and Picot went to Petrograd, the Russians, who had extensive ecclesiastical establishments in the Holy Land and who had at the

s by Leila F. Wilson except as noted.

Haram al-Sharif, showing Dome of the Rock with Mount of Olives to the left.

La vue d'un tel monument est comme une musique continuelle et fixée.

MME. DE STAEL

Richard Cleave

Aerial view of the city showing Kidron and Hir Valleys and Mount Zion.

Rooftops of the Walled City from roof of the convent on the supposed site of the Antonia Fortress of Herod the Great. Two Domes of Holy Sepulchre are on center skyline.

From the east, Jerusalem rises on the skyline
above the desert valley leading to the Dead Sea.

Crusader sculpture on the façade Church of the Holy Sepulchre.

Jews on their way to the Wailing Wall, 1940.

start of the talks asserted a claim to Palestine for themselves, agreed after some discussion to an international régime providing it covered the whole country, since many of their establishments were outside the Jerusalem-Bethlehem area.

The British did not inform the Sharif Husayn of Mecca of the Sykes-Picot Agreement, which is clearly incompatible with their promises to him. When the Bolsheviks revealed the existence of the Agreement, the Turks immediately approached Husayn with an offer of Arab autonomy in return for Arab withdrawal from the war, but this was rejected. Husayn continued to rely on the word of the British and particularly on messages which he received from them after the Russian disclosure and which certainly contained a large measure of dissimulation as to the Sykes-Picot Agreement.

Sources: The text of the Sykes-Picot Agreement is given in Hurewitz, *Diplomacy in the Near and Middle East,* and extracts are given in Antonius' *The Arab Awakening.* For a discussion of the background, see, *inter alia:* Antonius, *The Arab Awakening;* Khouri, *The Arab-Israeli Dilemma;* Elizabeth Monroe, *Britain's Moment in the Middle East;* and Barbara Tuchman, *Bible and Sword.*

Appendix D
President Roosevelt's April 5, 1945
Letter to King Ibn Saud

April 5, 1945

Great and Good Friend:

I have received the communication which Your Majesty sent me under date of March 10, 1945 in which you refer to the question of Palestine and to the continuing interest of the Arabs in current developments affecting that country.

I am gratified that Your Majesty took this occasion to bring your views on this question to my attention and I have given the most careful attention to the statements which you make in your letter. I am also mindful of the memorable conversation which we had not so long ago and in the course of which I had an opportunity to obtain so vivid an impression of Your Majesty's views on this question.

You will recall that on previous occasions I communicated to you the attitude of the American Government toward Palestine and made clear our desire that no decision be taken with respect to the basic situation in that country without full consultation with both Arabs and Jews. You will also doubtless recall that during our recent conversation I assured you that I would take no action, in my capacity as Chief of the Executive Branch of this Government, which might prove hostile to the Arab people.

It gives me pleasure to renew to Your Majesty the assurances which you have previously received regarding the attitude of my Government and my own, as Chief Executive, with regard to the question of Palestine and to inform you that the policy of this Government in this respect is unchanged.

I desire also at this time to send you my best wishes for Your Majesty's continued good health and for the welfare of your people.

FRANKLIN D. ROOSEVELT

His Majesty
    Abdul Aziz Ibn Rahman Al Faisal Al Saud,
      King of Saudi Arabia,
        Riyadh.

(*A Decade of American Foreign Policy, 1941-9*, Senate Committee on Foreign Relations, 1950: from *Department of State Bulletin*, October 21, 1946, p. 623: drafted by the present author.)

Appendix E

The Anglo-American Committee of Inquiry

The Anglo-American Committee of Inquiry was appointed in November 1945 with the following terms of reference:

1. To examine political, economic and social conditions in Palestine . . .
2. To examine the position of the Jews . . . in Europe . . .
3. To hear the views of competent witnesses and to consult representative Arabs and Jews on the problems of Palestine . . . and to make recommendations for . . . handling these problems . . .
4. To make such other recommendations . . . as may be necessary to meet the immediate needs arising under paragraph 2 above . . .

The British members of the Committee were Sir John Singleton, W. F. Crick, R. H. S. Crossman, Sir Frederick Leggett, R. E. Manningham-Buller, and Lord Morrison. The American members were Judge Joseph C. Hutcheson, Dr. Frank Aydelotte, Frank W. Buxton, Bartley C. Crum, James G. McDonald, and William Phillips. Including secretarial and research assistants and court reporters, the personnel totaled 38. There were two British and two American secretaries: I was one of the latter.

The Committee's report, dated April 20, 1946, made the following recommendations:

1. Since "Palestine alone cannot meet the emigration needs of the Jewish victims of Nazi and Fascist persecution," the two Governments should endeavor to find homes for all such displaced persons, in cooperation with countries all over the world.
2. 100,000 displaced Jews should be admitted immediately to Palestine.
3. Palestine should be neither a Jewish state nor an Arab state, and the form of government ultimately to be established should, under international guarantees, fully protect and preserve the interests in the Holy Land of Christendom and of the Moslem and Jewish faiths.
4. Until the hostility between Jews and Arabs disappears, any attempt to establish either an independent Palestinian State or independent Palestinian States would result in such strife as might threaten the peace of the world; therefore the Government should continue under mandate pending the execution of a trusteeship agreement under the United Nations.
5. The mandatory or trustee should prepare measures to bridge the gap between the Arab and Jewish standards of living.

151

6. The mandatory should continue to "facilitate Jewish immigration under suitable conditions" (in the words of the Mandate), while rejecting both the view that Jewish immigration should be conditioned upon Arab acquiescence and the view that Jewish immigration should "proceed apace in order to produce as quickly as possible a Jewish majority and a Jewish State."

7. The land transfer regulations of 1940 (restricting the sale of lands to Jews) should be rescinded, as should any provisions stipulating that only members of one community may be employed on the land.

8. Agricultural and industrial development on a large scale should be promoted.

9. The educational system of both Jews and Arabs should be reformed, to eliminate nationalistic propaganda and to improve the facilities for Arab education.

10. The Jewish Agency should resume cooperation with the mandatory in suppressing terrorism and illegal immigration and in the maintenance of law and order.

Sources: The report of the Committee was published by both governments (U. S. Government Printing Office, 1946 and Cmd. 6808, respectively). The maps published with the report are especially noteworthy. Three members of the Committee have written about the Committee's mission: R. H. S. Crossman, *Palestine Mission, a Personal Record*, New York: Harper and Brothers, 1947; Bartley C. Crum, *Behind the Silken Curtain*, New York: Simon and Schuster, 1947; and William Phillips, *Ventures in Diplomacy*, Boston: Beacon Press, 1952 (Chapter 24). See also an article on the Committee by the present author in the *American Foreign Service Journal*, v. 23, no. 7, July, 1946.

Appendix F

The Internationalization of Jerusalem, 1947-1950

The different proposals advanced over the years for the solution of the Palestine question by partition, such as the Peel (1937) and Woodhead Commission reports, as well as the UNSCOP majority reports, and indeed the Morrison-Grady plan for provincial autonomy, all recognized the need for giving some special treatment to Jerusalem, because of its unique character as the site of the Holy Places. This aspect was frequently mentioned when the General Assembly of the United Nations had the problem of Jerusalem before it in 1947, 1948, 1949 and 1950.

The 1947 partition resolution had a whole section devoted to the city of Jerusalem. The basic provision read: "The City of Jerusalem shall be established as a *corpus separatum* under a special international régime and shall be administered by the United Nations." The *corpus separatum* would comprise an area of some 100 square miles, with a population of about 210,000. Bethlehem and certain other suburbs were included in the proposed international zone (see map 2), which incidentally was the one which the foreign consuls always used, and still use, in defining the theoretical limits of their jurisdiction in Jerusalem. There was to be a governor appointed by and responsible to the Trusteeship Council and a legislative council elected by all adult residents. The Holy Places would be under the protection of the Governor.

The Trusteeship Council duly prepared a draft statute for the city in the spring of 1948, but this was not put into effect because by this time there had already been considerable fighting between Arab and Jewish forces in Jerusalem and the city was in effect divided (as it remained until June 1967). By the end of the fighting in the 1948 Palestine War, moreover, the Israelis had secured the Jerusalem corridor, which provided a connecting link between the Israeli-held portions of the city and the rest of Israel. This was a new and significant development. The UNSCOP majority report and the UN partition resolution had foreseen the international zone of Jerusalem as being wholly surrounded by the territory of the proposed Arab state. The fact that the dividing line between Arab-held and Israeli-held territory now ran right through Jerusalem made it more difficult to set up an international régime for the city, which, whatever the UN resolutions might say, did not form a separate enclave on the ground.

Count Folke Bernadotte, the UN Mediator, devoted considerable attention to the Jerusalem problem. His final report, submitted the day before his assassina-

153

tion in September 1948, recommended, *inter alia,* that there should be a special international régime for the city and also that there should be a United Nations conciliation commission to try to work out a solution to the basic issues in dispute between the parties. The General Assembly, in a resolution of December 11, 1948, established the Palestine Conciliation Commission (PCC), which incidentally is still in existence. Its members are the United States, France and Turkey. One of the tasks of the PCC was to be to prepare proposals for a permanent international régime for Jerusalem with "maximum local autonomy consistent with the special international status of the Jerusalem area." The boundaries of the international zone would be patterned after those of the 1947 partition plan.

In September 1949, the PCC produced a plan for Jerusalem which would have divided the city into Arab and Jewish zones, with considerable local autonomy and closely linked to Jordan or Israel, respectively. There would be a UN Commissioner who would be charged with protection of the Holy Places. The city would have a general council composed of equal numbers of Arab and Jewish members which would deal with matters of common interest. This plan got caught in the cross-currents that were beginning to develop in the General Assembly and elsewhere between the advocates of territorial and the advocates of functional internationalization.

By territorial internationalization is meant the placing of a specific piece of territory under international administration, as envisaged, for example, in the original United Nations partition plan (the *corpus separatum*). Functional internationalization, on the other hand, would place the Holy Places under some form of international protection, without setting up an actual international area. At this time, territorial internationalization was strongly supported by the Vatican (and hence by most Roman Catholic states) and also had the support of the Arab states with the important exception of Jordan, which wanted no international régime for the city at all. The functional approach tended to appeal to most Protestant countries and, in this period, to Israel.

When the Jerusalem problem again came before the General Assembly, in December 1949, neither the PCC plan nor a proposal submitted by the Netherlands and Sweden for functional internationalization won general acceptance. Instead, the Assembly reaffirmed its support for the concept of full territorial internationalization as provided in its original resolution of two years before, and again instructed the Trusteeship Council to prepare a plan for the city. Meanwhile, the Israelis went ahead with their plans to transfer their government departments from Tel Aviv to Jerusalem and the Knesset (Parliament) under date of January 23, 1950, proclaimed that Jerusalem was "once again" the capital of Israel. These Israeli actions were taken despite a formal undertaking given by Israel at the time of its admission to the United Nations (May 1949) that it would abide by the terms of the 1947 and 1948 resolutions, both of which of course provided for the internationalization of Jerusalem.

The Trusteeship Council met during the winter of 1949-50 and approved a statute for Jerusalem which its chairman was directed to discuss with the Israelis and Jordanians. The Statute, which covered the same area as the 1947 partition plan and was similar in most ways to the Trusteeship Council's earlier plan, was a detailed blueprint for territorial internationalization. It provided for a legislative council with membership divided equally among the three religions (Christian, Muslim and Jewish) and a UN governor.

In any event, the Jordanians declined to discuss any type of internationalization and went ahead with their plans to annex the West Bank, including the Old City (effective April 24, 1950). While the Jordanians did not go so far as to proclaim Jerusalem to be their capital, or to move their ministries there, they did later declare it to be Jordan's "second capital." The Israelis for their part informed the Chairman of the Trusteeship Council that they were unhappy about many features of the proposed Statute but would be agreeable to some form of functional internationalization of the Holy Places (almost all of which were in the Jordanian sector anyway).

The Trusteeship Council, in view of the attitudes of the two countries most closely involved, decided it could take no further action and so informed the General Assembly. When the matter came back to the Assembly, in December of 1950, Sweden again introduced a proposal for functional and Belgium a proposal for territorial internationalization. Neither resolution passed and that was the end of the Assembly's consideration of the Jerusalem issue, until after the June War.

By way of comment on this admittedly unsatisfactory outcome, it should be kept in mind that once the two halves of Jerusalem were physically separated it became extremely difficult to internationalize the city, particularly as each sector grew more and more linked economically to Israel or to Jordan. Thus the 1949 resolution of the General Assembly, calling again for the full territorial internationalization of so large an area as the *corpus separatum* and ignoring economic factors, was highly unrealistic. At that stage, functional internationalization of the Holy Places alone would have been more feasible, as it would have avoided taking the two sectors away from the jurisdiction of Israel or Jordan, respectively. Today, however, with the city again united, it should be easier to raise again the possibility of territorial internationalization, at least for some part of the area.

Sources: The story of the various proposals for the internationalization of the city is given in Khouri, *The Arab-Israeli Dilemma,* and in an unpublished Ph.D. thesis by H. Eugene Bovis, *The Jerusalem Question, 1917-1968.* An account of the PCC appears in Pablo de Azcárate, *Mission in Palestine, 1948-1952.* A critique of the plans for internationalization is to be found in Halpern, *The Idea of the Jewish State.* The text of the 1947 partition resolution may be found in Hadawi (ed.), *United Nations Resolutions on Palestine, 1947-1965,* and in many other sources.

Appendix G

Tripartite Declaration Regarding Security in the Near East

Three-Power Statement

(Released to the press May 25)

The Governments of the United Kingdom, France, and the United States, having had occasion during the recent Foreign Ministers meeting in London to review certain questions affecting the peace and stability of the Arab states and of Israel, and particularly that of the supply of arms and war material to these states, have resolved to make the following statements:

1. The three Governments recognized that the Arab states and Israel all need to maintain a certain level of armed forces for the purposes of assuring their internal security and their legitimate self-defense and to permit them to play their part in the defense of the area as a whole. All applications for arms or war material for these countries will be considered in the light of these principles. In this connection the three Governments wish to recall and reaffirm the terms of the statements made by their representatives on the Security Council on August 4, 1949, in which they declared their opposition to the development of an arms race between the Arab states and Israel.

2. The three Governments declare that assurances have been received from all the states in question, to which they permit arms to be supplied from their countries, that the purchasing state does not intend to undertake any act of aggression against any other state. Similar assurances will be requested from any other state in the area to which they permit arms to be supplied in the future.

3. The three Governments take this opportunity of declaring their deep interests in and their desire to promote the establishment and maintenance of peace and stability in the area and their unalterable opposition to the use of force or threat of force between any of the states in that area. The three Governments, should they find that any of these states was preparing to violate frontiers of armistice lines, would, consistently with their obligations as members of the United Nations, immediately take action, both within and outside the United Nations, to prevent such violation.

Source: Department of State Bulletin, June 5, 1950, p. 886.

Appendix H

The Eric Johnston Mission and the Problem of the Jordan Waters

Between 1953 and 1955, Eric Johnston, as the personal representative of President Eisenhower, made four trips to the Middle East in an effort to gain the assent of Israel and the Arab states to the so-called Unified Development Plan for the waters of the Jordan River. The plan had as its objective the orderly development of the water resources of the Jordan basin for the benefit of all four riparian states (Lebanon, Syria, Israel and Jordan). The basic premise was that the water resources of the Jordan were to be used within the Jordan Valley until the needs of all the land in the Valley for irrigation had been met. With this purpose in mind, the plan proposed specific allocations of water to each of the four riparian states.

An important feature of Johnston's proposals was that once the needs of all users in the Jordan basin itself were met, any participating state could use its allocation wherever it saw fit, *i.e.* outside the basin. This would have provided for Israel's National Water Carrier, by which Israel planned to take water from the upper Jordan (in amounts within its allocation) to the coastal plain and south.

After protracted negotiations by Johnston with representatives of the four countries involved, technical experts on the part of both the Arab states and Israel agreed to recommend his proposals to their governments. However, in October 1955, the Arab League Political Committee declined for political reasons to endorse the plan, and returned it to the Arab Technical Committee for further consideration. The main stumbling-block was that the plan would have involved some measure of collaboration with Israel, through a body of international engineers who would have supervised the execution of the plan, including carrying out of the proposed allocations of water, and who would presumably have been under the United Nations.

Since 1955, it can be said that the Unified Plan has been implemented unilaterally by the two principal users of the Jordan waters, Israel and Jordan, since they have conformed to its proposed allocations in taking water from the river. It can also be said that the Arab Diversion Plan, which would have carried the headwaters of the river around that portion of the river where Israel is a riparian state, and which was never completed, could hardly have been compatible with the objective of securing the "orderly" development of the water resources. Nor could the Israel Saline Effluent, a canal by which the Israelis have been releasing highly salt water from Lake Tiberias back into the river at the point where it enters Jordanian territory. The Unified Plan is still regarded by the United States government as the best attempt to deal with the waters question.

Sources: Eric Johnston's proposals are outlined, and the background discussed, in two pamphlets by Georgiana G. Stevens: *The Jordan River Valley*, International Conciliation (the Carnegie Endowment for International Peace) no. 506, January, 1956; and *Jordan River Partition*, Hoover Institution Studies 6, The Hoover Institution on War, Revolution and Peace, 1965. See also two articles by Yoram Nimrod in *The New Outlook*: "The Unquiet Waters," v. 8, no. 4 (July 1965) and "Conflict Over the Jordan," v. 8, no. 6 (September 1965).

Appendix I

The Joseph Johnson Mission and the Problem of the Arab Refugees

In 1961 and 1962, Dr. Joseph E. Johnson, President of the Carnegie Endowment for International Peace, was sent to the Middle East by the Palestine Conciliation Commission to discuss the Arab refugee problem with Israel and the four Arab "host countries": the UAR, Jordan, Syria and Lebanon. He put forward a set of proposals which would have combined an Israeli willingness to take back a certain number of refugees (never fixed) with Arab willingness to see the rest of the refugees permanently settled. The basis for Dr. Johnson's proposals was the UN General Assembly's resolution No. 194 (III) of December 11, 1948, paragraph 11 of which provided that the "refugees wishing to return to their homes and live at peace with their neighbors" should be permitted to do so and that compensation should be paid for the property of those choosing not to return.

An essential feature of Dr. Johnson's proposals would have been a poll of the refugees by which individuals would have an opportunity to express their preferences freely. His objective was to obtain not so much the formal agreement as the acquiescence of the governments involved. Negotiations broke down, however, when Israel declined to make a firm commitment about the return of some refugees, while the Arab states maintained their official position that all should return. Like the Johnston waters plan, the Johnson refugee plan is considered by the United States government to represent the best attempt to date to deal with an important aspect of the overall Arab-Israel problem.

Sources: Dr. Johnson made his proposals public in an address before the American Assembly at Arden House, Harriman, New York, released by the American Assembly October 24, 1963. See also The Middle East Journal, Summer, 1964, for text.

Appendix J

Statement by Ambassador Charles W. Yost, United States Representative to the United Nations, in the Security Council, on the Situation in Jerusalem, July 1, 1969

Once again the Council has been summoned to deal with certain actions taken by the Government of Israel in Jerusalem. We have listened carefully to the statements of the Permanent Representative of Jordan and other Arab Ambassadors, as well as the reply of the Representative of Israel.

The discussion thus far has made amply clear that the status of Jerusalem is not an isolated problem, but, rather, an integral part of a whole complex of issues in the current Middle Eastern conflict which must be resolved. This is not a novel conclusion. The Council clearly recognized that fact in Resolution 242, which treats the entire Middle Eastern situation as a package. This resolution remains the basis of our approach to a just and lasting peace in the area. You are all well aware of the strenuous efforts my own Government is making to help Ambassador Jarring promote a peaceful settlement. Progress in these efforts has, admittedly, been slow. This is perhaps not surprising when one reflects on how deep the roots of the conflict go. But the important thing is that some progress is being made. The fact that it has not been crowned with dramatic success should not give grounds for despair. Nor should it be exploited as justification for actions, which will make greater progress even more difficult. This applies to actions in Jerusalem as elsewhere in the area. Indeed, Jerusalem occupies a very special place in all our minds and all our hearts as one of the holiest cities in the entire world. For Jerusalem is a sacred shrine to three of the world's largest and oldest religious faiths: Islam, Christianity and Judaism. By virtue of the fact the United States has always considered that Jerusalem enjoys a unique international standing and that no action should be taken there without full regard to Jerusalem's special history and special place in the world community. Unfortunately there have been acts of many kinds which have broken the peace in Jerusalem and which are of deep concern to my Government and to the international community. Mr. President, we understand the deep emotional concerns which move all parties to the Arab-Israeli dispute on the subject of Jerusalem. We do not believe, however, that any of these concerns are served by what is now taking place in East Jerusalem, whether it be

160

actions by those now exercising authority there or by individuals considering themselves aggrieved and therefore justified in resorting to violence. The expropriation or confiscation of land, the construction of housing on such land, the demolition or confiscation of buildings, including those having historic or religious significance, and the application of Israeli law to occupied portions of the city are detrimental to our common interests in the city. The United States considers that the part of Jerusalem that came under the control of Israel in the June War, like other areas occupied by Israel, is occupied territory and hence subject to the provisions of international law governing the rights and obligations of an occupying power. Among the provisions of international law which bind Israel, as they would bind any occupier, are the provisions that the occupier has no right to make changes in laws or in administration other than those which are temporarily necessitated by his security interest, and that an occupier may not confiscate or destroy private property. The pattern of behavior authorized under the Geneva Convention and international law is clear: the occupier must maintain the occupied area as intact and unaltered as possible, without interfering with the customary life of the area, and any changes must be necessitated by immediate needs of the occupation. I regret to say that the actions of Israel in the occupied portion of Jerusalem present a different picture, one which gives rise to understandable concerns that the eventual disposition of East Jerusalem may be prejudiced and the rights and activities of the population are already being affected and altered.

My Government regrets and deplores this pattern of activity, and it has so informed the Government of Israel on numerous occasions since June 1967. We have consistently refused to recognize these measures as having anything but a provisional character and do not accept them as affecting the ultimate status of Jerusalem.

I have explained in some detail the opposition of the United States to certain measures taken by the Government of Israel in Jerusalem, since this is the precise object of the complaint brought before us by the Government of Jordan. But, as I suggested earlier, we cannot logically and intelligently consider the problem of Jerusalem without putting it in its proper perspective—the Middle East situation as a whole. In this connection, I would recall that one of the first major policy decisions taken by President Nixon after assuming office this year was that the United States Government should take new initiatives in helping to try to bring peace in the Middle East. For the past several months we have been devoting our best efforts to this task. We shall continue to do so but for these efforts to succeed we will require the goodwill and cooperation of the parties themselves. A just and lasting peace in the Middle East is long and tragically overdue. It will not be found through terror bombings, which inevitably harm innocent civilians, any more than through unilateral attempts to alter the status of Jerusalem. It will be found only through the instruments and processes of negotiation, accommodation and agreement. It will come only through the exercise by the parties of the utmost restraint—not just along the cease-fire lines or in public statements, but also on the ground in Jerusalem itself.

In treating the problem of Jerusalem, since we deal with it in the context of the total situation in the Middle East, my Delegation will subject any proposal for Council action, first of all, to the test of whether that proposal is likely to help or hinder the peaceful settlement process. I hope all members will do likewise. For example, one constructive move the Council might make would be to request the parties to lay aside their recriminations, to desist from any action— in Jerusalem or elsewhere—that might be construed as prejudicing or prejudging a final, comprehensive settlement a just and lasting peace. Thus, our consideration of the situation in Jerusalem could provide a fitting occasion on which to insist once more that the parties to a dispute which keeps the world's Holiest City in turmoil act responsibly to resolve the whole dispute and, until it is resolved, that they take no action anywhere which could further jeopardize its resolution.

Source: Press release USUN-70(69) July 1, 1969, United States Mission to the United Nations.

Bibliography

1. GENERAL AND HISTORICAL

Acheson, Dean. *Present at the Creation, My Years in the State Department.* New York: W. W. Norton, 1969.

Antonius, George. *The Arab Awakening.* London: Hamish Hamilton, 1938.

Avnery, Uri. *Israel Without Zionists.* New York: Macmillan, 1968.

Badeau, John S. *The American Approach to the Arab World.* New York: Harper and Row, 1968.

Barbour, Neville. *Palestine, Star or Crescent?* New York: Odyssey Press, 1947. (Published in England as *Nisi Dominus;* reprinted 1969 by Institute of Palestine Studies, Beirut).

Crossman, Richard. *Palestine Mission.* New York: Harper and Brothers, 1947.

Crum, Bartley C. *Behind the Silken Curtain.* New York: Simon and Schuster, 1947.

Davis, John. *The Evasive Peace.* London: John Murray, 1968.

DeNovo, John A. *American Interests and Policies in the Middle East 1900-1939.* Minneapolis: University of Minnesota, 1963.

Eban, Abba. *My People.* New York: Behrman House and Random House, 1968.

Eddy, William A. *F.D.R. Meets Ibn Saud.* New York: American Friends of the Middle East, 1954.

Friedmann, Georges. *The End of the Jewish People?* (Translated from the French) New York: Doubleday, 1967.

Frischwasser-Ra'anan, H. F. *Frontiers of a Nation.* London: Batchworth, 1955.

Gervasi, Frank. *The Case for Israel.* New York: The Viking Press, 1967.

Graves, R. M. *Experiment in Anarchy.* London: Victor Gollancz, 1949.

Hadawi, Sami. *Bitter Harvest.* New York: The New World Press, 1967.

Halperin, Samuel. *The Political World of American Zionism.* Detroit: Wayne State University Press, 1961.

Halpern, Ben. *The Idea of the Jewish State.* Cambridge: Harvard University Press, 1961. Reprinted, 1969.

Hertzberg, Arthur (ed.). *The Zionist Idea.* New York: Doubleday, 1959.

Herzl, Theodor. *The Jewish State.* (Translated from the German.) New York: American Zionist Emergency Committee, 1946.

Hodes, Aubrey. *Dialogue with Ishmael.* New York: Funk and Wagnalls, 1968.

Howard, Harry N. *The King-Crane Commission.* Beirut: Khayats, 1963.

Hull, Cordell. *Memoirs.* New York: Macmillan, 1948.

Hurewitz, J. C. *The Struggle for Palestine.* New York: Norton, 1950.

Jeffries, J. M. N. *Palestine, the Reality.* London: Longmans Green & Co., 1939.

Khouri, Fred J. *The Arab-Israeli Dilemma.* Syracuse: The University Press, 1968.

Lawrence, T. E. *Seven Pillars of Wisdom.* London: Jonathan Cape, 1926.

163

Lenczowski, George, ed. *United States Interests in the Middle East.* Washington: American Enterprise Institute, 1968.

Marlowe, John. *The Seat of Pilate.* London: The Cresset Press, 1959.

McDonald, James G. *My Mission in Israel.* New York: Simon and Schuster, 1951.

Millis, Walter, ed. *The Forrestal Diaries.* New York: The Viking Press, 1951.

Monroe, Elizabeth. *Britain's Moment in the Middle East, 1914-1956.* London: Chatto and Windus, 1963.

Murphy, Robert. *Diplomat Among Warriors.* Garden City: Doubleday, 1964.

Nasser, Gamal Abdel. *The Philosophy of the Revolution.* Cairo: Mondiale Press, no date.

O'Ballance, Edgar. *The Arab-Israeli War, 1948.* New York: Praeger, 1957.

Peretz, Don C. *Israel and the Palestine Arabs.* Washington: The Middle East Institute, 1958.

Phillips, William. *Ventures in Diplomacy.* Boston: Beacon Press, 1952.

Polk, William R. *The United States and the Arab World.* Cambridge: Harvard University Press, 1965.

Polk, William R., David M. Stamler and Edmund Asfour. *Backdrop to Tragedy, the Struggle for Palestine.* Boston: Beacon Press, 1957.

Rodinson, Maxime. *Israel and the Arabs.* (Translated from the French.) New York: Pantheon Books, 1968.

Safran, Nadav. *The United States and Israel.* Cambridge: Harvard University Press, 1963.

————. *From War to War.* New York: Pegasus, 1969.

Sanger, Richard H. *Where the Jordan Flows.* Washington: The Middle East Institute, 1963.

Sharabi, Hisham. *Palestine and Israel, the Lethal Dilemma.* New York: Pegasus, 1969.

Stein, Leonard. *The Balfour Declaration.* New York: Simon and Schuster, 1961.

Stevens, Georgiana G. *Jordan River Partition.* Hoover Institution Studies 6. Stanford: The Hoover Institution on War, Revolution and Peace, 1965.

————. *The Jordan River Valley. International Conciliation* (The Carnegie Endowment for International Peace) No. 506, January, 1956.

————, ed. *The United States and the Middle East.* Englewood Cliffs: Prentice Hall, 1964.

Storrs, Sir Ronald. *Memoirs.* New York: G. P. Putnam's Sons, 1937 (published in Great Britain as *Orientations*).

Sykes, Christopher. *Crossroads to Israel.* London: Collins, 1965.

————. *Two Studies in Virtue.* London: Collins, 1953.

Truman, Harry S. *Memoirs.* Garden City: Doubleday, 1955.

Tuchman, Barbara W. *Bible and Sword.* New York: New York University Press, 1956.

Weizmann, Chaim. *Trial and Error.* Philadelphia: The Jewish Publication Society, 1949.

Yale, William. *The Near East.* Ann Arbor: University of Michigan Press, 1958.

Zeine, Zeine. *The Emergence of Arab Nationalism.* Beirut: Khayats, 1966.

2. JERUSALEM AND THE HOLY PLACES

Bovis, H. Eugene. *The Jerusalem Question, 1917-1968.* Unpublished Ph.D. dissertation. Washington, The American University, 1968.

Cragg, Kenneth. *The Call of the Minaret.* New York: Oxford University Press, 1956.

————. *Sandals at the Mosque.* London: S.C.M. Press, 1959.

Curzon, Robert. *Visits to Monasteries of the Levant.* London: John Murray, 1881.

Elliot, Elisabeth. *Furnace of the Lord.* Garden City: Doubleday, 1969.

Guillaume, Alfred. *Islam.* Baltimore: Penguin Books, 1954.

Hoade, Eugene. *Guide to the Holy Land.* Jerusalem: The Franciscan Press, 1962.

Hollis, Christopher, and Ronald Brownrigg. *Holy Places.* New York: Praeger, 1969.

Joseph, Dov. *The Faithful City.* New York: Simon and Schuster, 1960.

Kendall, Henry. *Jerusalem, the City Plan.* London: H. M. Stationery Office, 1948.

Khalidi, Walid. *Jerusalem: The Arab Case.* Amman: Hashemite Kingdom of Jordan, 1967.

Kollek, Teddy, and Moshe Pearlman. *Jerusalem, a History of 40 Centuries.* New York: Random House, 1968.

Matthews, Charles D. *Palestine, Mohammedan Holy Land.* New Haven: Yale University Press, 1949.

Moore, Elinor A. *The Ancient Churches of Old Jerusalem.* Beirut: Khayats, 1961.

Perowne, Stewart. *The Pilgrim's Companion in Jerusalem and Bethlehem.* London: Hodder & Stoughton, 1964.

————. *The One Remains.* London: Hodder & Stoughton, 1954.

Pfaff, Richard H. *Jerusalem, Keystone of an Arab-Israeli Settlement.* Washington: American Enterprise Institute, 1969.

Rackauskas, Constantine. *The Internationalization of Jerusalem.* Washington: The Catholic Association for International Peace, 1957.

Rosenthal, Gabriella and Werner Braun. *Jerusalem.* Garden City: Doubleday, 1968.

Steckoll, Solomon. *The Gates of Jerusalem.* New York: Praeger, 1968.

Vester, Bertha. *Our Jerusalem.* Garden City: Doubleday, 1955.

Williams, Albert N. *The Holy City.* New York: Duell, Sloan and Pearce, 1954.

3. THE UNITED NATIONS IN PALESTINE
(see section 5 for United Nations publications)

Azcárate, Pablo de. *Mission in Palestine.* Washington: The Middle East Institute, 1966.

Bernadotte, Folke. *To Jerusalem.* London: Hodder & Stoughton, 1951.

Burns, E. L. M. *Between Arab and Israeli.* London: Harrap, 1962; reprinted in paperback, Beirut: Institute for Palestine Studies, 1969.

Hutchison, E. H. *Violent Truce.* New York: Devin-Adair, 1956.

Von Horn, Carl. *Soldiering for Peace.* London: Cassell, 1966.

4. THE JUNE WAR

Churchill, Randolph S. and Winston S. *The Six Day War.* London: Heinemann, 1967.

Donovan, Robert J., ed. *Six Days in June: Israel's Fight for Survival.* New York: Signet Books, 1967.

Draper, Theodore. *Israel and World Politics.* New York: The Viking Press, 1968.

Kimche, David and Dan Bawley. *The Sandstorm.* New York: Stein and Day, 1968.

Laqueur, Walter. *The Road to Jerusalem.* New York: Macmillan, 1968; reprinted in paperback as *The Road to War,* a Pelican book, Baltimore: Penguin Books, 1969.

MacLeish, Roderick. *The Sun Stood Still.* New York: Athenaeum, 1967.

Marshall, S. L. A. *Swift Sword.* New York: American Heritage Publishing Co., 1967.

Prittie, Terence. *Israel—Miracle in the Desert.* New York: Praeger, 1968.

Vance, Vick, and Pierre Lauer. *Hussein of Jordan: My "War" with Israel.* New York: Mirror, 1969.

5. DOCUMENTS

Hadawi, Sami, ed. *United Nations Resolutions on Palestine, 1947-1965.* Beirut: Institute for Palestine Studies, no date.

Hurewitz, J. C. *Diplomacy in the Near and Middle East* (a collection of documents). Princeton: Van Nostrand, 1956.

Laqueur, Walter. *The Israel-Arab Reader* (a collection of documents). New York: The Citadel Press, 1968.

Magnus, Ralph H., ed. *Documents on the Middle East 1969.* Washington: American Enterprise Institute, 1969.

Great Britain. *Palestine, Royal Commission, Report.* London: H. M. Stationery Office, 1937 (Cmd. 5479). Peel Report.

————. *Palestine, Partition Commission, Report.* London: H. M. Stationery Office, 1938 (Cmd. 5854). Woodhead Report.

————. *Statement of Policy on Palestine, May 17, 1939.* (Cmd. 6019). The White Paper.

Palestine, Government of. *A Survey of Palestine,* prepared for the Anglo-American Committee of Inquiry. Jerusalem: The Government Printer, 1946.

————. *The Political History of Palestine Under British Administration,* prepared for the United Nations Special Committee on Palestine. Jerusalem: The Government Printer, 1947.

————. *A Supplementary Memorandum* to the United Nations Special Committee on Palestine. Jerusalem: The Government Printer, 1947.

United Nations, *Special Committee on Palestine, Report to the General Assembly.* Lake Success, 1947. (Partition report).

United Nations, *General Assembly,* Resolution No. 181 (II), November 29, 1947. (Partition of Palestine).

————, ————, Resolution No. 194 (III), December 11, 1948. (Establishment of Conciliation Commission).

————, ————, Resolution No. 303 (IV), December 9, 1949. (International Régime for Jerusalem).

————, ————, "The Situation in the Middle East." A letter to the Secretary General from the Permanent Representative of Jordan to the UN. A/7084, April 19, 1968. (The Desecration of Christian Cemeteries and Church Property in Israel).

————, ————, "The Situation in the Middle East." A letter to the Secretary General from the Permanent Representative of Jordan to the UN. A/7092, May 1, 1968. (A demonstration by Arab women against the holding of the Israeli military parade).

————, *Security Council.* Provisional Verbatim Record of the 1347th meeting, S/PV. 1347, and Supplemental Information received by the Secretary General, S/7930, both dated June 5, 1967. (Expulsion of General Bull from Government House).

———, ———. Report of the Secretary General under General Assembly Resolution 2254 (ES-V), Relating to Jerusalem, S/8146, September 12, 1967. (Thalmann Report).

———, ———. Report of the Secretary General under General Assembly Resolution 2252 (ES/V) and Security Council Resolution 257 (1967), Relating to Populations under Israeli control, S/8158, October 2, 1967 (Gussing Report).

———, ———. Letter to the Secretary General from the Permanent Representative of Israel to the UN. S/8439, add. 1, March 6, 1968. (Desecration of Jewish sites in Jordan).

———, ———. Provisional Verbatim Record of the 1421st meeting. S/PV1421, May 3, 1968. (Statement of Mr. Rouhi Al-Khatib, Mayor of Jerusalem).

———, ———. Addendum. S/PV1421, add. 1, May 3, 1968. (Documents mentioned by Mr. Al-Khatib in his statement).

United States, Department of State. Anglo-American Committee of Inquiry, Report to the United States Government and His Majesty's Government in the United Kingdom. Lausanne, Switzerland, April 20, 1946. Washington: US Government Printing Office, 1946. (Also issued by HMG as Cmd. 6808).

———, ———. American Foreign Policy, Basic Documents, 1950-55. Dept. of State publication 6446, General Foreign Policy Series 117, released July, 1957.

———, ———. American Foreign Policy, Current Documents, 1956, 1957 and 1958, in same series.

———, ———. Policy in the Near East Crisis. Dept. of State Publication 8269, Near and Middle East series 75, released August 1967, revised July 1969.

———, Senate Committee on Foreign Relations. A Decade of American Foreign Policy, 1941-1949. Washington: US Government Printing Office, 1950.

———, ———. A Select Chronology and Background Documents Relating to the Middle East, June 6, 1967. Washington: US Government Printing Office, 1967. First Revised Edition, May 1969, issued by US Government Printing Office, 1969.

6. ARTICLES

Badeau, John S. "The Arabs—1967." The Atlantic Monthly, December, 1967.

Darin-Drabkin, Haim. "Jerusalem, City of Dissension or Peace?" New Outlook, Vol. 11, no. 1, January, 1968.

Hourani, Cecil. "The Moment of Truth." Encounter, November, 1967.

Jones, S. Shepard. "The Legal Status of Jerusalem: Some National and International Aspects." Law and Contemporary Problems, XXXIII, No. 1, (Winter, 1968).

Laqueur, Walter Z. "Is Peace in the Middle East Possible?" New York Times Magazine, August 27, 1967.

Leary, Byron V. "An UNTSO Executive's View." Mideast (published by the American Friends of the Middle East), September, 1968.

Peretz, Don C. "Jerusalem: A Divided City." Journal of International Affairs, XVIII, No. 2, 1964.

———. "A Binational Approach to the Palestine Question." Law and Contemporary Problems, XXXIII, No. 1.

———. "The Arab-Israel War: Israel's Administration and Arab Refugees." Foreign Affairs, Vol. 46, No. 2, January, 1968.

Roosevelt, Kermit. "The Partition of Palestine, a Lesson in Pressure Politics." Middle East Journal, Vol. II, No. 1, January, 1948.

Sanders, A. J. "Urbis et Orbis: Jerusalem Today." *The Christian Century,* July 26, 1967.

Schleifer, Abdullah. "The Fall of Jerusalem." *The Evergreen Review,* December, 1967.

Stevens, Georgiana. "Jerusalem—1968." *Vista* IV, No. 1, July-August, 1968.

Swados, Harvey. "The Bridge on the River Jordan." *New York Times Magazine,* November 26, 1967.

Yost, Charles W. "How the Arab-Israel War Began." *Foreign Affairs,* January, 1968.

——. "Israel and the Arabs: The Myths that Block Peace." *The Atlantic Monthly,* January, 1969.

Index

169

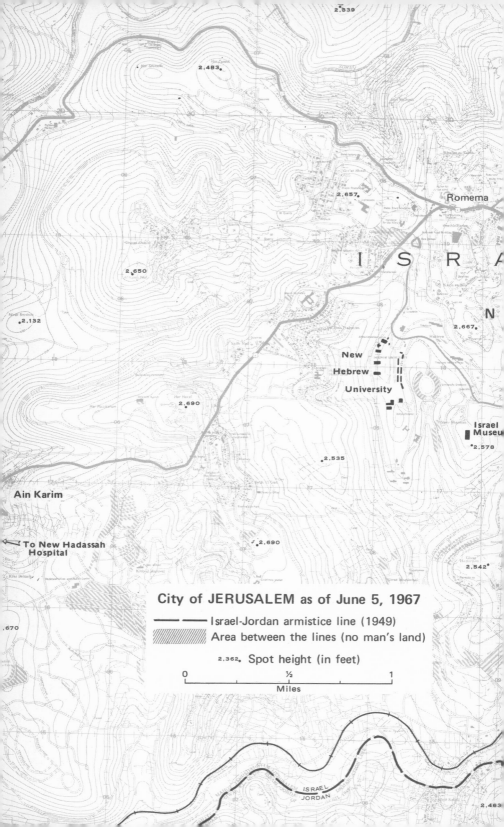

City of JERUSALEM as of June 5, 1967

—— —— Israel-Jordan armistice line (1949)

//////// Area between the lines (no man's land)

2.362. Spot height (in feet)

0 — — — ½ — — — 1
Miles